THE PEMBROKESHIRE GUIDE

by **Brian John**

Foreword by Lord Parry of Neyland

AF470246

GREENCROFT BOOKS

FOREWORD

There could be no finer "guide" to Pembrokeshire than Dr. Brian John himself. This man who speaks in our broad vowelled accents has studied his native peninsula more closely than any other of his contemporaries. He has devoted his scholarship and his life to it. He knows Pembrokeshire. It is in his blood, in his bones, in his scholarship.

Having acted as a guide to television audiences and radio listeners and written books on the basic geography of West Wales, he returned from the classroom to his best loved field of study and has lived what we now call "the good life" on the hills of Presely and the beaches that run around St. Bride's Bay.

While he is as sentimental as any other Pembrokeshire man or woman in his love of his down below childhood, he approaches his work with a trained scientific mind and any reader can be certain that the truth within the legend is exposed without stripping off the mysticism and the mystery that is so much a part of the magic of "gwlad yr Hud", the magic mystic land of Non the mother of St. David and St. David himself.

It is a delight to write a foreword to a guide prepared by such a distinguished son of Pembrokeshire.

Lord Parry of Neyland
Past Chairman, Wales Tourist Board

A Note about Maps

Visitors who enjoy exploring the countryside are recommended to obtain at least one detailed topographical map of Pembrokeshire. There are a number of good car atlas maps available, and some of the touring maps published by petrol companies at the scale of 1 inch : 5 miles are excellent. Free maps published by the Wales Tourist Board are available from Tourist Information Centres; and the Bartholomew "Half-inch" series map of Pembroke is good, if somewhat dated in appearance. The most essential maps of all are the O.S. 1:50,000 folded maps, numbered 157 (St. David's and Haverfordwest), 158 (Tenby), and 145 (Cardigan). These maps are not cheap, but they are modern in appearance, reasonably up-to-date as far as information is concerned, and easy to use. Get to know the grid reference system if you can; without it you may well fail to find many of the delightful localities mentioned in this book!

CONTENTS

WELCOME TO PEMBROKESHIRE

The ancient county of Pembrokeshire disappeared - in theory at least - with the reorganization of local government in 1974. But as a region with its own very distinct character, Pembrokeshire still exists. It is more beautiful, more interesting, and more varied than the other component parts of the new county of Dyfed, and both local people and visitors identify strongly with this "land of magic and enchantment" which occupies a far-flung peninsula in the Celtic Sea.

This little guide-book, the first comprehensive guide to Pembrokeshire for many years, has been written in order to provide up-to-date and reliable information to the holidaymaker on a multitude of topics. Most of all, the author's intention in writing this book has been to enable holidaymakers to *enjoy* Pembrokeshire. This is a place to be experienced with all the senses, to be relished and to be cherished.

Here there are truly magnificent landscapes, so many and so diverse that authors almost without exception have expressed their amazement that such variety can be encompassed within such a small area. In the north we find the bleak open moorlands and the coniferous woodlands of the Presely Hills. In the west the little city of St. David's occupies part of a windswept plateau some 200 feet above sea-level, with bare rocky hills such as Carnllidi and Penbiri looking more like mighty mountain ranges when seen from a distance against the evening sky. In the centre of Pembrokeshire the fertile and well-wooded valleys of the Eastern Cleddau and Western Cleddau rivers give a gentler aspect to the landscape, and the deep sheltered inlet of Milford Haven brings the influence of the sea deep into the heart of the region. In the south the limestone terrain of the Castlemartin Peninsula is well-drained and fertile, once famous for rich harvests of corn and for black cattle, but nowadays used as a Ministry of Defence tank range.

Pembroke Millpond and Castle

Fringing this land of infinite variety is the glorious Pembrokeshire coast, with spectacular cliff scenery, islands rich in wildlife, small tidal creeks and spacious sandy beaches. The coastline, long renowned for its beauty, was recognized as a national scenic resource through the designation of the Pembrokeshire Coast National Park in 1952. The National Park covers an area of 225 square miles; most of the protected area lies within 3 miles of the sea, and no part of the Park is more than 10 miles from the coast. The entire length of the coastline is followed by the 180-mile Long Distance Coast Path, starting near St. Dogmael's in the north-east and ending at Amroth in the south-east. The only gaps in the path occur in the Milford Haven area and in the western part of the M.O.D. tank range. Only in the Fishguard area and in Tenby and Saundersfoot does the path run through urban environments, although the intrepid long-distance hiker will pass a number of coastal villages on the walk along the whole length of the coastline.

Pembrokeshire is renowned for its wildlife, and the coastal districts in particular are noted for their profusion of plant and animal communities. With so many different habitats available to plants, it is not surprising that there are tremendous contrasts in the colour and texture of vegetation between the woodlands and moorlands, the estuarine mud flats and the exposed cliff coast, and the sand dunes and sheltered creeks and coastal valleys. There are flowers everywhere - snowdrops and primroses in the early spring, sea-campion, thrift, bluebells and kidney vetch in the late spring and early summer, and a succession of other flowers during the high summer. May and June are the most colourful months, and the visitor to the cliff tops and hedgerows of Pembrokeshire at this time will carry away memories of sheets of brilliant colour and of the air heavy with perfume. And throughout the year the bright yellow gorse is in bloom, even when snow lies on the ground. Sea-birds are at their most numerous during the nesting season. From early April onwards razorbills, guillemots, puffins, kittiwakes, gulls and fulmars crowd into their traditional nesting places on the Pembrokeshire islands and on places on the mainland also. Grassholm is the site of a vast gannet colony, while Manx Shearwaters occupy many thousands of breeding burrows on the islands of Skomer and Skokholm. Grey seals abound in the coastal waters, breeding during the autumn on remote beaches and in caves above the reach of storm-waves.

Scenery, wildlife and sandy sunlit beaches are by no means the only holiday resources of Pembrokeshire. Much of the old county's special charm is related to the rich legacy of historical features, dating from prehistoric to modern times, which are to be found on all sides. Among the most spectacular features are the cromlechau or burial chambers dating from Neolithic times, and the Iron Age hill forts and other settlement sites which are often asssociated with ancient fields bounded by rough stone walls. There are abundant traces of the "Age of the Saints" (450-800 AD), during which St. David and other missionaries introduced Christianity and stimulated a great flowering of Celtic culture. However, the most profound impact upon the landscape was made by the Normans and their followers, who arrived in Pembrokeshire in 1094. They conquered and then colonised the greater part of the region, creating over 100 new villages, constructing first motte and bailey castles, then mighty stone fortresses, and even building fortified towns like Tenby, Pembroke and Haverfordwest. Many of the churches of Pembrokeshire also date from this period of colonial rule, and it was in the twelfth and thirteenth centuries that "Little England beyond Wales" became a distinct cultural region, separated from the Welshry of North Pembrokeshire by an invisible line that came to be called the Landsker.

Many of the farm buildings and stately homes of Pembrokeshire date from the seventeenth and eighteenth centuries, and in spite of much rebuilding within the last 200 years there are abundant

SCOLTON MANOR MUSEUM

The Museum about Pembrokeshire

Ideal for a rainy day!

and Country Park
On B4329, 5½ miles North of Haverfordwest
Telephone: Clarbeston 328
OPEN: June - September 10.30 a.m. - 6.00 p.m.
Tuesday to Sunday – Admission Charge.
Picnic Sites, Free Car Parks, Refreshments.
A day out for all the family.

PENRHOS COTTAGE
Llanycefn, Nr. Maenclochog
(Map Ref. SM 102258)
Traditional Thatched Welsh Home – near Gors Fawr Stone Circle
OPEN: Easter and May - September
10 - 12.30 and 2.30 - 6 p.m.
Closed Mondays and Sunday Morning.

CASTLE MUSEUM & ART GALLERY
The Castle, Haverfordwest. Tel: 3708
Origins of the Town, Military Museum, Art and other Exhibitions. Admission Charge.
Open all year 10 - 5.30 p.m. (11 - 4 p.m. Winter)
Tuesday to Saturday. Free Car Park.

Milford Haven oil tanker

fascinating buildings in the towns and countryside of Pembrokeshire which provide clues to a rich history of economic and social changes. Most of the little stone quays and jetties of the outer coastal creeks and the "inland" ports (i.e. those of Milford Haven and the tidal creeks of the Daugleddau waterway) date from the days of the sailing ships, but in Fishguard, Milford Haven, Neyland and Pembroke Dock there are signs of much later seafaring activities with the coming of the railways in the mid-1800's, and the dreams of Brunel and others concerning trans-Atlantic passenger traffic. Pembroke Dock was, in the early years of this century, the site of the world's most advanced royal naval dockyard. Other traces of the "industrial revolution" in Pembrokeshire are to be found on the Pembrokeshire Coalfield, where iron-making, coal mining and coal exporting were all important local activities, and elsewhere in the region where abandoned quarries and mines are to be discovered in the most unexpected of places. Then there are the modern industries of Pembrokeshire, represented in particular by the oil installations of Milford Haven - oil refineries, deep-water ocean terminals, storage tanks, and the gigantic Pembroke Power Station. Maybe these installations, and the oil tankers which serve them, are not the stuff of which holiday picture postcards are made, but they add yet another element to the already immensely varied Pembrokeshire scene.

Whatever your taste as a holidaymaker - whether it be sunbathing or windsurfing, natural history or archaeology, walking or sailing, industrial archaeology or castle-hunting, fishing or exploring forgotten railways, eating good food or browsing in craft workshops and museums - Pembrokeshire will provide what you need. Luckily, although road and rail access is now excellent, the old county is still not overcrowded even at the height of the holiday season. The beaches provide room to relax, and the roads are almost always clear enough for you to take your car and explore at will. One word of advice. Pembrokeshire covers an area of only 614 square miles, and you may be tempted the "do" the whole region in the space of a week or a fortnight. If you try this you are likely to suffer from shell-shock. Instead, take it easy. Relax in your own favourite way for part of your holiday and explore just some of the areas described in this book. There is so much to see and experience that you will inevitably end your holiday with a rich storehouse of memories. Then, next summer or on an "out-of-season" break, come back and sample some other parts of Pembrokeshire. The locals are renowned for their friendly hospitality, and there are thousands of families who are so "hooked" on Pembrokeshire that they return year after year to their own private hiding-places and to meet old friends.

So - welcome to Pembrokeshire! Have a wonderful time, and come and see us again!

INFORMATION DESK

The information below has been compiled from a variety of sources. In particular, acknowledgement is made to Preseli District Council, South Pembrokeshire District Council and the *Western Telegraph* and *Tivyside Advertiser* newspapers. Additional information comes from the publications of the Pembrokeshire Coast National Park Department. Since addresses, opening hours and telephone numbers can change, no responsibility can be taken for errors in the listings below; readers are advised to check information with either the local newspapers or with tourist information centres.

Emergency Services

Ambulance: Pembrokeshire ambulance centre, Haverfordwest 3347. In emergency dial 999.
Police: County Headquarters, Carmarthen 236444 for normal service. Other stations: Fishguard 873225; Haverfordwest 3355; Milford Haven 2351; Neyland 600221; Narberth 860389; Pembroke 682121; Saundersfoot 812223; St. David's 720223; Tenby 2303. In emergency dial 999.
Fire: Fire prevention advice - normal working hours: Haverfordwest 2131. In emergency dial 999.
Coastguard: St. Anne's Head, Dale 218. In emergency dial 999.
Gas: Tenby 3251 or Skewen 815678 (for area north of St. David's/Maenclochog).
Electricity: Haverfordwest 3305 or Carmarthen 236761 (for Cardigan area).
Water: Haverfordwest 3881.
Dyfed C.C. Surveyors: Carmarthen 236641.

How not to dress for a 7 mile walk in the Presely Hills.

Hill Safety Code

- ★ Wear clothing which is colourful, warm, wind-proof and waterproof. Even if the weather is hot and settled, take extra clothing with you in your rucksack.
- ★ Wear walking boots or stout shoes in the hills.
- ★ Be prepared for emergencies - even in the Presely Hills you can get lost, so carry map, compass, watch, torch and spare batteries, whistle, first-aid kit, high-calory food rations and a large polythene bag for cover. Accidents can happen even in high summer when the weather is warm.
- ★ Plan your route carefully and make sure someone knows where you are going and when you expect to be back. Stick to your intended route. Never walk alone and don't split up except in an emergency.
- ★ Watch the weather - cloud and rain can transform the Presely Hills even in summer. If you are lost in the cloud, look for a safe way off the hills. Generally it is best to descend to the south.
- ★ If there is thunder about, get off the hills as quickly as possible.
- ★ Follow local advice about weather and conditions on the Presely ridge.

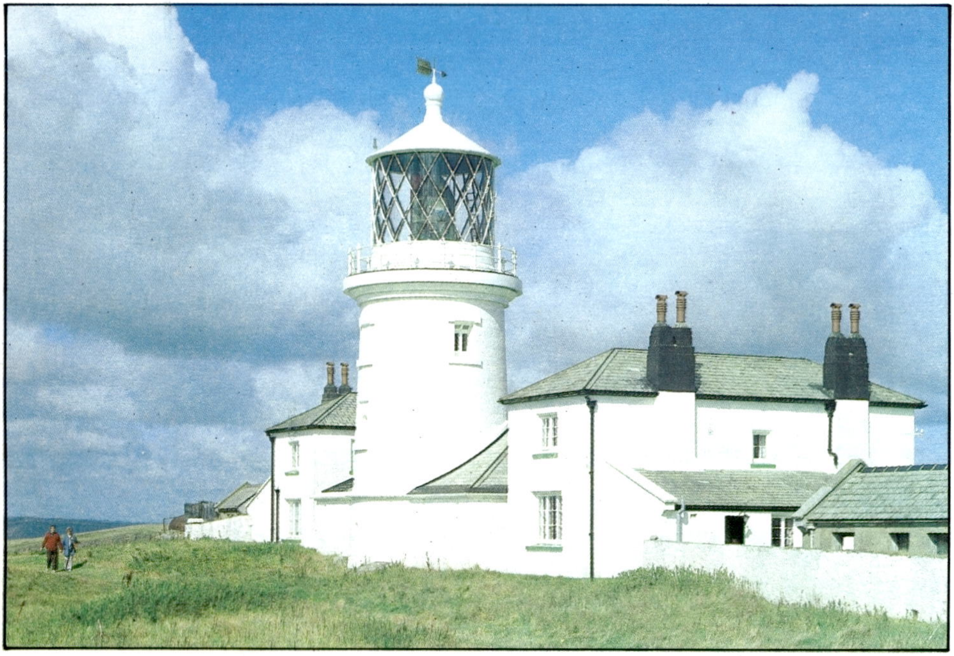

The Lighthouse on Caldey Island

PUBLIC TRANSPORT IN DYFED

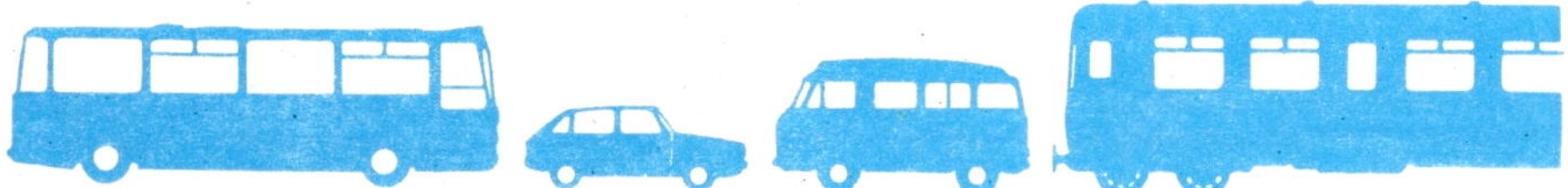

Dyfed is a beautiful County, and has a wide range of scenic attractions varying from coast to mountains. You'll be surprised at how many of these places you can reach using regular public transport services.

If you would like more details, call in at a Tourist Information Centre and collect a free Public Transport Map of the area, or contact the County Council's Transportation Section, at the address below. For information on particular services get in touch with the relevant operators in your area. Whether you're a resident, or simply visiting, why not take advantage of the special offers and discount deals available all year round ?

Remember that from a bus or train you can see so much more of the countryside. No worries, no traffic jams, no parking problems - give it a try !

Car drivers deserve a break as well - let someone else do the driving and have a proper holiday.

Dyfed County Council
Highways & Transportation Dept.
Llanstephan Road
CARMARTHEN SA31 3LZ
Telephone:
Carmarthen (0267) 233333

CYNGOR SIR
DYFED
COUNTY COUNCIL

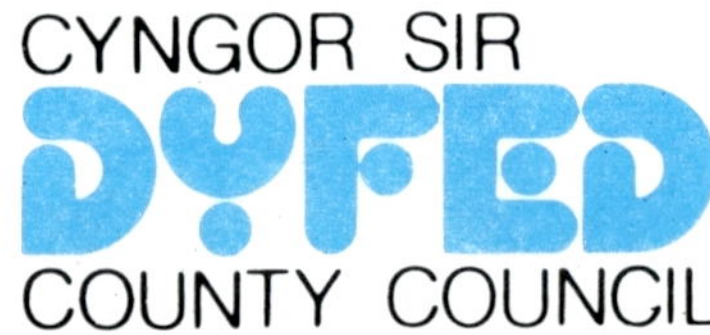

Transport

The Cleddau Bridge

Trains: British Rail weekdays and Sundays, Fishguard 872881; Haverfordwest 4361; Swansea 467777; Tenby 2248; Whitland 240322.
Buses: Cleddau Bus and Coach Station, Haverfordwest 3284. Richards Bros. Moylgrove Garage, Cardigan 613756. Silcox Motor Coach Company Limited, Pembroke 683143 and Tenby 2189.
Car Breakdowns: AA Service Centre, Kilgetty (Saundersfoot 812896).
RAC Service Centre, Kilgetty (Saundersfoot 813321).
A 24-hour car breakdown service is also provided by the following garages:–
Green Bower Garage, Slebech (Rhos 251)
Johns Bros. Garage (Manorbier 485)
Pembroke Sand Co. Ltd. (Pembroke 682864 or 684077)
R.C. Freeman (Milford Haven 2145 or 2410)
Llangoedmor Motor Body Repairs (Cardigan 612947 or Llechryd 476)

Health and Safety

Hospitals
Visiting times for hospitals which serve the area: Cardigan & District (Cardigan 612214): 2 p.m.-8 p.m. every day
South Pembrokeshire (Pembroke 682114): 2 p.m.-8 p.m. every day.
St. David's (Carmarthen 237481): every evening 5.45 p.m.-6.45 p.m. Wednesday, Saturday, Sunday 2.15 p.m.-3.25 p.m.
Tenby Cottage (Tenby 2040): 2 p.m.-8 p.m. every day.
West Wales General (Carmarthen 235151): Visiting times vary from ward to ward and according to day of the week. Contact the hospital for details. For record requests on Radio Glangwili please ring Carmarthen (0267) 235843 between 8 p.m. and 10 p.m., Sunday to Friday, or 8 a.m. to 12 noon on Saturday.
Withybush (Haverfordwest 4545): 7 p.m.-8 p.m. every day. Saturday, Sunday 2.30 p.m.-3.30 p.m. For record requests on Hospital Radio Withybush telephone Haverfordwest 67196, 24-hour answering service.

Doctors and Health Centres
There are doctors in most of the towns and larger villages of Pembrokeshire, and weekly surgeries are held in some of the smaller settlements also.
The main health centres are as follows:–
Cardigan: The Health Centre (Tel: 612837).
Fishguard: The Health Centre (Tel: 873041).
Haverfordwest: The Health Centre, Merlins Hill (Tel: 3345).
Milford: The Health Centre, North Road (Tel: 3366).
Milford: The Health Centre, Observatory Ave., Hakin (Tel: 2236).
Narberth: The Health Centre, Northfield Road (Tel: 860206).
Newport: The Health Centre, Long Street (Tel: 820397).
Neyland: The Health Centre, Charles Street (Tel: 600268 or 600582).
Pembroke: The Health Centre, East Back (Tel: 682344).
Pembroke Dock: The Health Centre, Park Street (Tel: 682635).
Saundersfoot: Westfield Road, Saundersfoot (Tel: 812407).
Tenby: The Health Centre, Greenhill (Tel: 4161/2).
The Health Centre, Warren Street (Tel: 2991).
(**Note:** for Dentists and Opticians see the local Yellow Pages Directory.)

Chemists on Duty

Below are the usual times (outside normal shop hours) during which prescriptions can be dealt with by local dispensing chemists in the main towns. Chemists work on a rota system; check the local press for details of duty chemists during any particular week. In smaller towns and villages (e.g. Newport and Crymych) opening times are normally notified on the door of the chemist concerned.

Cardigan: (Mon.-Fri. 6-7, Weds. 2-3 p.m.; Sunday 11 a.m.-12 noon).
Fishguard: (Mon.-Fri. 5.30-6.30 p.m.; Sun. 11 a.m.-12 noon).
Haverfordwest: (Mon.-Fri. 6-7 p.m.; Sun. 11.30 a.m.-12 noon).
Milford Haven: (Mon.-Fri. and Sun. 5.30 -6.30 p.m.).
Narberth: (Weekdays exc. Weds. 6-6.30 p.m.; Weds. 5.30-6.30 p.m.; Sun. 11.30-12.30 p.m.).
Pembroke: (Mon.-Fri. 5 -6 p.m.; Weds. 6-7 p.m.; Sun. 12 noon-1 p.m.).
Pembroke Dock: (Mon.-Fri. 6-7 p.m.; Sun. 11.30 a.m.-12.30 p.m.).
Tenby: (Mon.-Fri. and Sun. 5.30-6.30 p.m.).

DID YOU KNOW ...

that Tenby is the sunniest resort in Wales and that Dale is even sunnier?

DID YOU KNOW ...

that Pembrokeshire has its own herd of red deer (raised for venison) on a farm at Esgyrn, not far from Fishguard?

that Pembrokeshire has its own peculiar variety of daffodil called the Tenby Daffodil?

that Woodstock Chapel (built 1754) not far from Ambleston, is a very imprtant symbol of the Methodist Revival, being the first Methodist Chapel not to be consecrated by a bishop?

that a coypu, who must have been very lonely, was caught in a garden in Abercych in 1949?

that there was a herd of feral goats on the cliffs and steep slopes of Dinas Island until 1947?

Voluntary Organizations

Alcoholics Anonymous: Milford Haven 5555. Fishguard 873024.
Al. Anon: Help for families of problem drinkers. Fishguard 873024, Johnston 890506.
Anorexic Aid: Dee Summons, Haverfordwest 2983.
British Diabetics Association: Pembroke 684704.
Citizens' Advice Bureau: 19a Meyrick Street, Pembroke Dock. Monday, Tuesday, Thursday, 10 a.m.-2 p.m.; Wednesday 10 a.m.-12 noon; Friday 10 a.m.-4 p.m. Pembroke 683805. Magistrates Court, Market Hall, Tenby, Tuesdays 10 a.m.-12 noon. National Westminster Chambers, 4 High Street, Cardigan. Monday-Friday 10 a.m.-1 p.m. Cardigan 613707.
Community Health Council: Picton House, 2 Picton Place, Haverfordwest. Tel: 5816 with 24-hour answering service. Public meetings, third Monday each month (except August). Speaker available.
Life Organisation: Free Pregnancy Testing and Support Group for Problem Pregnancies and Care. Tel: Haverfordwest 67242.

Haverfordwest Sports Centre

Queensway
Haverfordwest
Dyfed
Tel: Haverfordwest 5901

Bad Weather!

The Kids are bored!

Get them out of your hair for a while.
Go shopping!
Relax!

Send them to the Centre for organised activities.

Morning and afternoon sessions
Let us have your hassle!

Gingerbread: Meet at Pembroke Community Centre, Commons Road, Pembroke from 10.30 a.m. to 12 noon every Wednesday. All single parents welcome. For contact ring Pembroke 686463, Lamphey 672174 or Neyland 600576.
Marriage Guidance Council (Dyfed): See Telephone Directory for nearest appointment secretary.
Pembrokeshire Blind Organiser: Mr. Edmund Thomas, The Retreat, New Road, Freystrop, Haverfordwest. Tel: Johnston 890514.
Pembrokeshire National Deaf Children's Society: Secretary, Mr. G. Wheeler, 8 Cricket Grove, Hundleton. Tel: Pembroke 686976.
NSPCC: Group Office, Swansea 41795.
Pembrokeshire Multiple Sclerosis Society: For information ring Caroline Spencer, Llanteg 2351 or Iris Hinds, Saundersfoot 813264.
Samaritans: 6 Tower Hill, Haverfordwest, 11 a.m.-11 p.m. Haverfordwest 5536 or 66699. 11 p.m.-11 a.m. phone Swansea (0792) 55999.
Women's Aid Group: Counselling and Refuge, Tel: Haverfordwest 66699 to obtain rota number.
Women's Royal Voluntary Service: (including Country Cars Scheme): Lower Probation Office, Tower Hill, Haverfordwest. Entrance by Swimming Pool. Monday to Friday 9.30 a.m.-12.30 p.m.; 1 p.m.-3 p.m. Haverfordwest 2911.
R.S.P.C.A.: Carmarthen 233954.
Tenby Animal Rescue Centre: Tel: Tenby 3712.
Royal British Legion: (Ex-Service Welfare). County Branch Secretary, Mr. Vivian Morgan. Tel: Letterston 840427.
Soldiers, Sailors and Airmen's Families Association (SSAFA): Looks after the Forces' families. Tel: Manorbier 269.
Solo Plus: One Parent Family Support Group. Phone Madox 404 or Velindre 370 for information about meetings.
Pembroke and District Toy Library: Pennar Play School, Treowen Road, Pennar, Pembroke Dock. For children with special needs. Every Thursday 10 a.m. to 12 noon.

VOLUNTARY ORGANIZATIONS DIRECTORIES

Directory of Local Societies in Pembrokeshire, Dyfed County Library, Pembroke Region (1976).
The Dyfed Directory: Dyfed Rural Council (March 1981).
Voluntary Organizations Register: Preseli District Council (1982).

Shopping

Early Closing Days

Cardigan	Wednesday
Carmarthen	Wednesday
Haverfordwest	Thursday
Tenby	Wednesday
Saundersfoot	Wednesday
Narberth	Wednesday
Pembroke & Pembroke Dock	Wednesday
Fishguard	Wednesday
Kilgetty	Saturday
Milford	Thursday
Neyland	Wednesday
Newport	Wednesday

Market Days

Cardigan	Saturday, Monday (cattle)
Carmarthen	Saturday. Wednesday (cattle)
Haverfordwest	Saturday, Tuesday (cattle)
Narberth	Every 2nd Thursday (cattle)
Pembroke & Pembroke Dock	Friday (cattle)
Fishguard	Thursday
Kilgetty	alternate Monday
Milford	Friday

Note: Tenby market, Cardigan market and the new Riverside market in Haverfordwest are normally open for a full six days per week.

Note: The main shopping centres mentioned above have a wide range of excellent shops. However, remember that "village shops" are still very much a part of the Pembrokeshire scene. These little shops need your support, for they help to keep rural communities alive in more senses than one!

PEMBROKE YEOMAN

Hill Street, Haverfordwest

Beer Garden ☆ Bar Lunches
Sunday Lunches ☆ Real Ale

For Lunch Bookings
Telephone 2500

Sea fishing on a Pembrokeshire beach

HISTORIC LAUGHARNE

Dylan Thomas's "Beguiling Island of a Town"

and for Welsh Crafts, Books, Handknits, Wool
and Old Maps and Prints
you will find

oriel evans

adjacent to Brown's Hotel

Open 7 days in season
Telephone: Laugharne 635

A romantic Victorian portrayal of Lydstep Caverns

Odds and Ends

Cycle Hire

Bicycles can be hired on a daily or weekly basis from the following:–
Cross Inn Garage, Broadmoor, Kilgetty (Saundersfoot 813266).
Port Tack, The Strand, Saundersfoot (Saundersfoot 812212).
Newport Garage, Bridge Street, Newport (Newport 820305).
Rent-a-cycle, City Garage, Nun Street, St. David's.

Newspapers

Cardigan & Tivyside Advertiser, 39 St. Mary Street, Cardigan (weekly Thursdays) (Tel: 612513)
County Echo, West Street, Fishguard (weekly Tuesdays) (Tel: 872179)
Tenby Observer, South Parade, Tenby (weekly Fridays) (Tel: 3262)
West Wales Guardian, 18 Market Street, Haverfordwest (weekly Thursdays) (Tel: 2357)
Western Telegraph, Press Buildings, Merlin's Bridge, Haverfordwest (weekly Wednesdays) (Tel: 2551)

Local Authority Offices

Dyfed County Council, County Hall, Carmarthen (Tel: 233333)
Preseli District Council, Cambria House, Haverfordwest (Tel: 4551)
South Pembrokeshire District Council, Llanion Park, Pembroke Dock (Tel: 683122)
(Various Departments and Area Offices have other addresses and telephone numbers. Details can be found in the Telephone Directory).

Libraries

High Street, Fishguard (Tel: 872694)
Guildhall, Cardigan (Tel: 612578)
St. Peter's Street, Carmarthen (Dyfed County Library H.Q.) (Tel: 230873)
Dew Street, Haverfordwest (Regional Library H.Q.) (Tel: 2070)
Hamilton Terrace, Milford Haven (Tel: 2892)
St. Clements Road, Neyland (Tel: 600791)
Meyrick Street, Pembroke Dock (Tel: 683336)
Greenhill House, Tenby (Tel: 3934)
There are also smaller branch libraries at: Narberth, Newport, St. David's, St. Dogmael's.

Coastal Safety Code

★ When walking on cliff paths take extreme care, especially on windy days and when the ground is wet.
★ Look out for the effects of fresh coastal erosion - new collapsed cliff sections, rock falls and unmarked sheer drops.
★ Do not allow children to run or walk ahead of you on clifftop paths.
★ On beaches beware of the effects of a rising tide - do not walk to places where you may be cut off from a safe exit.
★ When bathing, beware of strong currents and beware of the effects of undertow when there is heavy surf.
★ Never bathe or swim alone.
★ Never allow children to bathe or swim without supervision, even when the sea is calm.
★ Get to know the characteristics of a beach before entering the water - most beaches are safe but some are not. See pp. 86-91.
★ Never bathe immediately after strenuous exercise.
★ Do not enter the water if a red flag is flying.
★ If you see two red and yellow flags on a beach, bathe between them, since this is the area patrolled by lifeguards.
★ Never remain in the water when cold.
★ Swim parallel to the shoreline and keep within your depth.
★ Air beds, rubber rings, tyres and rubber dinghies can be swept out to sea by winds and tides. Don't use them - they are potentially lethal.
★ When making a boat trip, make sure someone ashore knows where you are going and roughly how long you will be.
★ *If you see anyone in trouble telephone 999 and ask for the Coastguard.*

How not to behave on the coastal footpath.

Holiday Information

In recent years there has been a great improvement in the quality of information services in Pembrokeshire, with participation by the Wales Tourist Board, the South Wales Tourism Council, Dyfed County Council (and especially its National Park Department), and the two district councils of Preseli and South Pembrokeshire. The main local authority tourist information offices are as follows:

Dyfed County Council: Mr. Gerwyn Morgan, County Information Officer, Dyfed C.C., County Hall, Carmarthen (Tel: 0267-233333).

Pembrokeshire Coast National Park Dept.: Mr. Peter Hordley, Information Officer, National Park Dept., County Offices, Haverfordwest (Tel: 0437-4591).

Preseli District Council: Mr. Richard Howells, Public Relations and Tourism Officer, Preseli D.C., Cambria House, Haverfordwest (Tel: 0437-4551).

South Pembrokeshire District Council: Mr. David Pratt, Tourism Officer, S. Pembs. D.C., Tourist Information Centre, The Croft, Tenby (Tel: 0834-2402).

The County Council and National Park Information Offices provide information of a general nature, while the two district council offices can provide accommodation lists and a wide range of publicity and promotion materials.

Tourist Information Centres

Broad Haven: National Park Information Centre, Car Park, Broad Haven (Tel: 412).
Spacious and well-appointed information centre with permanent exhibits specialising on sea-shore and marine topics. Lab facilities are available. Also a wide range of books, maps and other materials on sale. A venue for evening lectures in and out of the holiday season. Open throughout the year. Ample car-parking space and also room for coaches. The Broad Haven Youth Hostel is next door.

Cardigan: Tourist Information Centre, Prince Charles Quay, Cardigan (Tel: 613230).
The best source of information about southern Ceredigion, the lower Teifi Valley and north-east Pembrokeshire. Bed-booking service operated by the Mid-Wales Tourism Council. No car-parking facilities.

Fishguard: Tourist Information Centre, The Town Hall, Market Square, Fishguard (Tel: 873484).
No room for permanent exhibits here, but the centre is bustling with life and has a friendly, efficient staff. Some literature on sale and hundreds of free leaflets about local accommodation, craft workshops and places of interest. Bed-booking service operated by the South Wales Tourism Council. No car-parking facilities.

Haverfordwest: National Park Information Centre, 40 High Street, Haverfordwest (Tel: 66141).
Permanent displays and a wide range of free leaflets and books and booklets for sale. Covers a wide area of central Pembrokeshire, including areas outside the National Park. Bed-booking service operated by the South Wales Tourism Council. No car-parking facilities.

Kilgetty: Tourist Information Centre, Kingsmoor Common, Kilgetty (Tel: Saundersfoot 813672/3 or 812175).
A spacious and well-designed centre with a display area, an information desk and a roomy café. Ample car-parking space and room for coaches to pull in. Leaflets, books and booklets about south Pembrokeshire in particular. Bed-booking service operated by the South Wales Tourism Council. Open all year round.

Newport: National Park Information Centre, Long Street, Newport (Tel: 820912).
A small information centre located conveniently adjacent to the town's main car-park. Attractive and informative photographic displays. Books, booklets, maps and National Park leaflets on sale; also many free leaflets about accommodation, craft workshops and visitor attractions.

Pembroke: National Park Information Centre, Drill Hall, Main Street, Pembroke (Tel: 682148).
No adjacent car-parking, but not far from the town's main car-park. Interesting displays relating to castles and fortifications. Open summer only. Full range of National Park publications on sale.

St. David's: National Park Information Centre, City Hall, St. David's (Tel: 720747).
One of the smaller centres, but with informative displays concentrating on St. David's and the surrounding area. Centrally located, but no car-parking facilities.

Tenby: Tourist Information Centre, The Croft, Tenby (Tel: 3510 or 2402).
A spacious information complex. The centre is well located, overlooking the North Beach. Excellent displays with audiovisual presentations etc. Staffed all the year round for enquiries, and during the summer it is a goldmine of essential information. Bed-booking service in cooperation with the Kilgetty centre. No car-parking facilities.

Accommodation

The bulk of holiday accommodation in Pembrokeshire is located - not surprisingly - within the National Park. On a typical August day there may be 130,000 visitors staying in Pembrokeshire, and during the course of the season well over a million holidaymakers enjoy the special delights of this area. The great majority of holidaymakers nowadays stay in self-catering accommodation - either in cottages and flats or else in static caravans. Of the remainder, about 10% of visitors stay in hotels, 6% in touring caravans, 5% in guest houses, 9% in tents, and 4% each in bed and breakfast accommodation and in farmhouse accommodation. The average length of stay is about 10 days - not nearly long enough for visitors to get to know the area! On the other hand we know that many families return to Pembrokeshire year after year, either to their old familiar haunts or moving each year to a new holiday base.

Nobody knows how many establishments there are in Pembrokeshire which take paying guests, but there must be many hundreds of them. They cater for all tastes and all pockets, and information about them can be obtained from Wales Tourist Board publications such as *Where to Stay in Wales* (the most comprehensive of all the accommodation guides, with compact information on each hotel, guest house etc., accompanied by colour photographs and classified by town). The annual *Bed and Breakfast* guide is also useful. In addition, the district council publications (namely *Preseli: the Heart of Pembrokeshire* and the *South Pembrokeshire Holiday Guide*) contain numerous advertisements for accommodation of all types. There are also accommodation lists, updated every year, from the two district councils and from the Fishguard, Goodwick and District Tourist Association, the Tenby and South Pembrokeshire Hotels and Restaurants Association, the Newport and District Chamber of Trade and Tourism, the Preseli Tourist Association, the St. David's Peninsula Tourist Association, and various Chambers of Trade. Agency lists of self-catering accommodation are available from Coastal Cottages of Pembrokeshire, Howells Holidays, Powells Cottage Holidays, Frank B. Mason & Co., Charles Birt & Co., King Thomas, Lloyd-Jones and Co., and various other firms. The Wales Tourist Board operates a number of schemes designed to ensure minimum standards at hotels, guest houses, flats and cottages, farmhouse accommodation centres and caravan parks. WTB publications have dragon symbols for all establishments which have received the Farmhouse Award, the Self-Catering Award or the Dragon Award (for caravan parks). These awards do of course guarantee high standards at appropriate establishments chosen by holidaymakers; but visitors should be aware that equally high standards are often to be found at establishments which do **not** hold these awards, since not all proprietors approve of the awards procedure.

Visitors to Pembrokeshire are strongly advised to complete their booking arrangements **before** arriving in Pembrokeshire. However, in case of problems over bookings, or where last-minute decisions are made to visit Pembrokeshire, the TIC's listed above can provide invaluable help. Two services are particularly important: the bed-booking service operated at the Tourism Council centres (Kilgetty, Haverfordwest, St. David's, Fishguard and Cardigan) and the Holiday Hotline service for last-minute bookings. Holiday Hotline can be contacted on Swansea 474308, and the Tourism Council centres also act as links for personal or telephone callers. There are district council Holiday Hotlines on 0437-66774 (for Preseli District) and on 0834-2402 (for Tenby, Saundersfoot and South Pembrokeshire).

Carnllidi by Jane Grigson

ST. NON'S HOTEL

St. Davids – Pembrokeshire
Telephone: St. Davids 720239

The Hotel is situated on the outskirts of St. Davids, overlooking the Cathedral. Within easy reach are wide sandy beaches, sheltered coves and beautiful cliff walks.

We are especially well known for exceptional food and service. All rooms have private bathroom, colour T.V., teasmade and telephone.
Special Bargain Breaks available
July and September included.

Write for Brochure and Tariff to:
Sandy Falconer, Proprietor
or telephone St. Davids (0437) 720239

DID YOU KNOW ...

that the Royal Dockyard at Pembroke Dock was, for most of the nineteenth century, the most technically advanced shipbuilding yard in the world?

that the islands of Skokholm and Skomer hold between them the world's largest concentration of shearwaters, probably totalling 135,000 pairs?

that Haverfordwest's Priory Ruins are haunted by a spectral monk who appears from time to time wearing his habit and cowl?

that the people of the Gwaun Valley in north Pembrokeshire still celebrate the Old New Year (locally called Hen Galan) on January 13th each year?

PEACE AND QUIET BESIDE THE SEA

at

BROAD HAVEN CARAVAN PARK

You can own your own Holiday Home only two minutes' walk from Broad Haven's safe golden sands. We offer a wide range of modern, fully serviced Holiday Homes on our peaceful and well maintained 'Dragon Award' Park.

A friendly welcome awaits you, so please telephone or call on Andrew or Eric Mock (Park Proprietors) for further details.

Telephone:
Broad Haven (0437 83) 277.

The South Pembrokeshire Holiday Coast Information Centre

at
The Croft, Tenby
(overlooking North Beach)
Telephone: (0834) 2402

let us help you
to see the best of South Pembrokeshire

The Green Bridge of Wales

Caravan Sites

There are over 300 caravan sites in Pembrokeshire, providing space for almost 9,000 caravans. About half of the sites are in the National Park, and these sites contain 61% of all caravans. The greatest concentration of caravans (both static and touring) is to be found in the south-east corner of Pembrokeshire around Tenby, Saundersfoot, Kilgetty and Amroth. Other popular areas for caravan holidays are around St. David's, Newgale and Fishguard. On an average August day there may be 29,000 people staying in static caravans in Pembrokeshire, with a further 7,000-8,000 in touring vans. The NPA believes that there are adequate sites for static caravan holidays, and visitors will find ample information concerning sites, hire charges, and booking procedures in tourist information centres and tourist accommodation guides. Standards in the main static caravan parks are improving all the time, and many are advertised as holders of the Wales Tourist Board "Dragon Award". This means that at least 50% of the caravans on site have shower or bath, inside WC, fridge, mains electricity and water, and heating at no extra charge. The best sites will have paved pathway access to each caravan, gardens and lawns, and parking adjacent to each caravan. The larger sites have their own swimming pools, club houses, shops and children's play areas. But remember that exotic facilities are not necessarily prerequisites for happy holidays; sites with 200-500 caravans can be noisy places with constant music and constant activity (even at the dead of night!), and many confirmed caravan holidaymakers prefer small sites in deeply rural settings where friendly, personal service from the proprietors more than compensates for a lack of facilities. Some sites without the Dragon Award have better facilities than those with it, and they attract the same families year after year.

Touring caravans are not immensely popular with local planners since they create problems of congestion on narrow Pembrokeshire roads and cause irritation especially when parked on roadside verges or public parking places overnight. However, touring caravanners have just as much right to holidays in Pembrokeshire as everybody else, and when they show consideration both on and off the road they cause little disturbance. They also bring a great deal of income to places like Newport and Marloes where there is a shortage of static caravan and hotel accommodation. Most touring caravanners will be aware of the locations of Caravan Club sites, but there are now 40 or more farm sites within the National Park alone where short stays by touring vans are possible. There are many others in the interior of Pembrokeshire. Short stays are possible at these sites, but because many of them take tents as well, and because new rules have recently come into force, it is difficult to generalise about the availability of space. The new rules make it possible for farmers and smallholders in a wide range of locations to take up to five caravans or tents at each site, although Caravan Club certified sites can take up to eight units. Intending visitors are advised to join the Caravan Club, to do their basic research on itineraries and sites before arriving in Pembrokeshire, and to book site places in advance. If you turn up at the entrance of a touring van site during the high season with no booking you will probably be turned away; maximum numbers on touring sites are now very strictly enforced by the NPA and by the other local authorities. Site operators will, if their site is full, attempt to find space for you elsewhere, but please bear in mind that if you drive around aimlessly late on a summer evening in the vague hope of finding an empty space on a farm site you will probably be disappointed. You will also make a lot of people very angry, especially if you happen to be driving along narrow Pembrokeshire lanes! If you need help in finding space, contact one of the TIC's listed on page 15. The staff have full lists of sites and may know where there are vacant pitches. In emergencies there are "transit touring sites" at Kilgetty and Carew for those who are lost in the wilderness with nowhere to go.

Camping Sites

There are probably at least 100 sites in Pembrokeshire where camping is permitted. Many of these are listed in WTB and other accommodation guides, and as noted above there are many farms with small touring sites where tents can be given space. On a typical August day there are now more people under canvas than there are in touring caravans, and perhaps 10% of all Pembrokeshire holidaymakers belong to the camping fraternity. Camping is cheap and nowadays relatively comfortable, so the popularity of camping holidays is increasing. However, the local authorities are not keen to see a great increase in camping holidays in Pembrokeshire because campers do not spend much money locally, because tents tend to be unsightly and conspicuous, and because camp sites can have severe problems of refuse and litter collection. Also, on some farm sites toilet and fresh water facilities can be inadequate, with consequent risks for public health. In particular, the authorities frown upon "wild camping" by both hikers and holidaymakers with their own cars, since trespass and wildlife disturbance are common problems. So, if you intend to take a camping holiday in Pembrokeshire, and if you do not belong to the Camping Club, please find out which registered sites are available and use them wherever possible. Guidance as to site facilities and prices can be obtained from

A million miles from city life ...

DRUIDSTONE HOTEL & ACTIVITY CENTRE

Climb a Pembrokeshire cliff, canoe round the coast, land yacht on the beach or try out field archery or surfing.

Informal Hotel that caters for outdoor people, isolated in 20 acres of cliff top grounds above beautiful quiet beach on National Park coast path.

Interesting international food from fresh natural produce and a well stocked Bar.

Hotel and self-catering Cottages. Children of all ages are welcome (unaccompanied from 11 years).

Write or telephone Jane Bell at Druidstone Hotel, nr. Haverfordwest, Dyfed

Tel: Broad Haven (043783) 221

EDUCATIONAL HOLIDAYS FOR ALL

Orielton is a delightful Georgian Manor House set in 120 acres of its own secluded woodland, south of Pembroke. Fully residential courses in all aspects of natural history, landscape and scenery, rambling, fishing, diving, photography and painting. Bed, breakfast, evening meal and packed lunch, plus all tuition fees and local transport £125 per week. Non-residents welcome on a daily basis.

For full programme of courses, contact Dr. Robin Crump, Orielton Field Centre, Pembrokeshire SA71 5EZ

Telephone: Castlemartin (064 681) 225

TIC's, and their staff can often help with last minute bookings. You are strongly advised to work out your touring schedule and make your site bookings *before* you arrive in Pembrokeshire. If you are walking the Coastal Footpath, the NPA can help by recommending camp sites at regular intervals around the coast; but bear in mind that there are a number of long coastal stretches which have *no* registered camp sites.

Youth Hostels and Field Centres

Pembrokeshire's youth hostels provide cheap and generally comfortable accommodation especially for hikers or other short-stay visitors. They are available only to members of the YHA, and during the peak holiday period they are very crowded. Advance booking is a necessity except at quieter times of the year. The Pembrokeshire hostels are somewhat irregularly spaced, as follows:

Poppit Sands, St. Dogmael's (40 beds). Tel: Cardigan 612936
Trevine (32 beds). Tel: Croesgoch 414
Pwllderi (26 beds). Tel: St. Nicholas 233
Whitesands Bay, St. David's (40 beds). Tel: St. David's 720345
Broad Haven (60 beds). Tel: Broad Haven 688
Marloes (40 beds). Tel: Dale 257
Pentlepoir, near Saundersfoot (34 beds). Tel: Saundersfoot 812333

Since the Newport hostel closed a few years ago attempts have been made by the YHA to find another site in or near the town, without success. Consequently there is a "gap" of 36.7 miles on the coastal footpath between the Poppit Sands hostel and that at Pwllderi. However, this should not discourage walkers who have doubts about their long-distance capabilities; there are adequate bed and breakfast and farmhouse accommodation establishments in the Newport-Dinas area, as well as small guest houses and camping sites. Walkers are strongly advised to obtain copies of the following leaflets by the NPA: *Coast Path Mileage* (10p) and *Coast Path Accommodation* (40p). They are worth their weight in gold, and will add hardly at all to your rucksack load.

There are two field study centres in Pembrokeshire owned and operated by the Field Studies Council. Both of these - at Orielton near Pembroke and at Dale Fort near the mouth of Milford Haven - specialise in marine biology residential courses, but resident staff members also run courses on a wide range of academic and non-academic subjects. The centres are available for individual and group bookings on either a serviced or self-catering basis. For part of the year they are heavily used by school and college groups, but during the holiday season many fascinating courses are put on for holidaymakers as "special interest" weeks. For further details ring Dale 205 (for Dale Fort) or Castlemartin 225 (for Orielton).

Wrought iron balconies, Haverfordwest

AIR SERVICE IN WALES
WELSH AIRWAYS
LIMITED

VISIT
HAVERFORDWEST AIRPORT
for
Pleasure Flights – Flying Lessons
Aircraft Hire – Picnic Park
Lunch or Dinner
HAVERFORDWEST 67979

Pembrokeshire Fly Fishers

Red House, Llawhaden
Narberth SA67 8DH

SALMON
AND SEA TROUT FISHING
SHOOTING
HOLIDAY FARMHOUSE
Llawhaden (09914) 252

Tide Tables

Tide tables for the summer months are readily available throughout the area, calculated for British Summer Time. Normally the tables are computed for Milford Haven.

Using the Milford Haven data as a basis, add or subtract as follows:–

Dale – 5 mins.
Fishguard or Goodwick + 68 mins.
Lawrenny + 10 mins.
Little Haven + 7 mins.
Neyland + 6 mins.
Pembroke Dock + 5 mins.
Porthstinian (St. David's) + 5 mins.
St. Dogmael's + 90 mins.
Solva + 10 mins.
Tenby – 12 mins.

Note: Low water times are approx. 6 hrs 10 mins after the times given for high water.

Note: The figures above, and the figures contained in the tide tables, are not to be looked on as 100% reliable. There can be considerable variations in both the height and time of high water, subject to prevailing wind conditions, the strength of tidal streams etc. So please be careful, especially when scrambling around the coast into remote creeks and bays.

Weather Forecasts

The "dial a weather forecast" service, operated by the National Park Department, is available every day throughout the summer months. This service comes from the Kilgetty Information Centre. If you dial Saundersfoot 812516 you will obtain (after 9.15 a.m.) a comprehensive local forecast, a note of the weather outlook, tide times for the day, and a listing of the day's walks and talks. If there is no reply dial direct to the Cardiff Weather Centre: Tel: 0222-397020.

SUMMER EVENTS

During spring, summer and autumn there are hundreds of events in Pembrokeshire which are of interest to the visitor. Many of these are "one-off" events, but others take place at approximately the same time every year. The list below gives some impression of the range of amusing, entertaining, fascinating and informative happenings which enliven the summer scene. You will find many more events advertised in the local press and in local tourist information centres. The most useful source of "events information" is the *What's On* leaflet published by the Dyfed Library Service and available from all library branches.

Approximate dates each year

May

Last Week: St. David's Bach Festival
Last Week: Newport Cnapan Festival Week
Spring Bank Holiday: Newport's Elizabethan Craft Fayre
Late: Saundersfoot Sailing Club, Coppet Hall Week.

June

Early: Tenby Golf Club Open Week
Mid: Saundersfoot Edwardian Week
Late: Gwyl Fawr (Eisteddfod), Cardigan
Late: Tenby Arts Festival Week

July

Early: Tenby in Bloom Week
Early: St. David's Craft Market
Mid: Milford Haven Carnival
Mid: St. Margaret's Fair, Tenby
Mid: Angle RNLI Regatta
Late: Brawdy RAF Air Day
Late: Fire Engine Rally, Haverfordwest
Late: Fishguard Music Festival
Late: Vintage Car Show, Scolton Manor
Late: Tenby Regatta
Late: Ffynnon Plant Steam and Vintage Rally
Late: Tenby Bowling Week

August

Early: Little Haven regatta
Early: Newport Craft Market
Early: Pembroke Agricultural Show
Early: Cardigan Agricultural Show
Early: Dale regatta
Early: Fishguard Agricultural Show
Early: Country and Game Fair, Scolton Manor
Early: Solva Regatta
Early: Nevern Show
Mid: Medieval Craft Fayre, Haverfordwest Castle
Mid: St. Dogmaels Regatta
Late: Saundersfoot Regatta
Late: Cilgerran Coracle Regatta
Late: Rowing and Longboat Races, Goodwick
Late: Tenby Horse Show
Bank Holiday: Newport Craft Market

Lamphey Palace.

ABOUT PEMBROKESHIRE

The Environment

Pembrokeshire is justly renowned for the beauty of its scenery and the fascinating variety of its rocks. Geology and landscape are closely interconnected, as we can see on the coast where in general the headlands are made of hard rocks and the bays of soft rocks or rocks broken by folding or faulting. The oldest of the region's rocks are of Precambrian age, over 1,000 million years old, while the youngest date from the Carboniferous period which ended about 295 million years ago. In general, the oldest rocks are to be found in north Pembrokeshire, and the youngest in the south. The best exposures of Cambrian rocks are to be found on the south coast of the St. David's Peninsula (Dewisland), and their greens, greys, purples and reds give the coastal cliffs an added interest. Ordovician sedimentary rocks underlie the land surface over most of north Pembrokeshire; these consist of shales, mudstones and sandstones, and they are often called "rab" by local people. Here and there, however, the sedimentary rocks are disturbed by great masses of igneous rocks - of volcanic origin - which have welled up from the earth's molten interior. These immensely hard rocks are in strips aligned broadly E-W or NE-SW, and they give rise to some of the most spectacular features of the local landscape. The rocky hills of Carnllidi and Penbiri near St. David's, the rough and rugged eminences of Pencaer near Fisguard, and the undulating uplands of Presely all owe their presence to these masses of Ordovician dolerite, diorite, gabbro and rhyolite.

In south Pembrokeshire the rocks are younger and the scenery is gentler. The overall structure is that of a broad basin, with the strip of Coal Measures (running across the region from St. Bride's Bay to Saundersfoot Bay) occupying the deepest part of the basin.

Three Very Luxurious Cottages

Three very luxurious Cottages for people who want somewhere special, on our 65-acre farm in the most beautiful part of North Pembrokeshire.

Welsh stone exterior, modern living inside. Dishwasher, colour T.V., all linen, private patio (and delicious meals available). Sorry, no pets.

Beaches, riding, fishing within easy reach. Featured in House & Garden, Cosmopolitan and The Good Holiday Cottage Guide.

AA Listed. Wales Tourist Board Self-Catering Award.

You are welcome to look around when you are in the area.

Colour Brochure from:
Mrs. Fay Cori
Fron Fawr
Boncath, Pembrokeshire
Dyfed SA37 0HS
Telephone: 023974 - 285

GLANHELYG
SUMMER
COURSES

- ☆ Improve your painting and drawing
- ☆ Experienced tutor
- ☆ Excellent accommodation in spacious Country House
- ☆ Large Studio
- ☆ Beautiful grounds with old walled garden, mature woods and stream
- ☆ In the Teifi Valley near beaches and Presely Hills
- ☆ Self-Catering Cottage
- ☆ Bring family or friend
- ☆ Opportunities to learn Pottery and other Crafts

For further details contact
Robin Holtom, M.A. (R.C.A.)
Glanhelyg, Llechryd
Nr. Cardigan, Dyfed SA43 2NJ
Telephone: (023987) 482

Submerged Forests

When the last remnants of glacier ice melted away at the end of the last glaciation, about 10,000 years ago, sea-level was much lower than it is now. Consequently, as the climate improved, peat-bogs and extensive woodlands developed offshore in many Pembrokeshire bays. About 8,000 years ago the woodlands consisted of oak, alder, hazel, birch and many other tree species, and there was abundant bird and animal life including wild pigs, deer, foxes and wolves, beavers and brown bears. Small tribes of Middle Stone Age people lived in forest clearings, using simple temporary shelters and obtaining their food supplies from trapped animals and birds, shellfish, nuts, berries and various edible plants. They spent part of their time on the shifting sandbanks of the coast and in river estuaries, but sea-level was rising inexorably, and gradually the woodlands and marshes were overwhelmed by the sea. For a few centuries the sea-level rise was as fast as 10ft. per century, and we can be sure that during severe storms great tracts of country were laid waste by coastal flooding. Now, with the sea holding steady at about its present level, the old offshore forests are submerged beneath sand, silt and pebbles. Occasionally, when winter storms lower the beaches in bays such as Newgale, Newport, Whitesands and Lydstep, the old forests can be seen again when the tide is low, and it is possible to examine in detail broken tree-stumps, branches, peat beds, and even deposits of hazel nuts and acorns which are over 7,000 years old.

On either side of the coalfield there are strips of older rocks - the Old Red Sandstone seen in the cliffs of Milford Haven, the Carboniferous Limestone of the Castlemartin Peninsula, and the Millstone Grit seen in the crumbling cliffs between Tenby and Monkstone Point. The great waterway of Milford Haven is cut right through the strips of these younger rocks - a deep, drowned river valley system on whose shores the creeks and bays reflect in detail the nature of the local geology.

Pembrokeshire was once part of the enormous Caledonian mountain range which stretched from the Arctic to the Tropics, and the alignment of this range can still be picked up in the arrangement of north Pembrokeshire rocks. But over the 400 million or so years that have elapsed since the creation of this mountain range the processes of erosion connected with water, wind, frost and ice have eroded away many thousands of feet of rock. Now Pembrokeshire is basically a lowland, except for the gentle swelling Presely ridge which is the last local remnant of the once-mighty Caledonian mountain range. The greater part of the Pembrokeshire land surface has been worn away by rivers and the sea (at times of higher sea-level) over the last 50 million years, with wave action responsible for the spectacular "coastal platforms" which are particularly characteristic of the St. David's Peninsula and the Castlemartin Peninsula between 100 and 200 feet above sea-level.

The "Sheep Dip" at Cenarth Falls

DID YOU KNOW ...

that Tenby is the sunniest resort in Wales and that Dale is even sunnier?

that the island of Skomer has its own unique subspecies of the common bank vole, called *Clethrionomys glareolus skomerensis*?

Further changes in the landscape can be dated to the last 2 million years or so - a period referred to by earth scientists as the Quaternary Ice Age. The landscape features created by snow, ice and glacial meltwater include Cwm Cerwyn on the flank of the Presely ridge, the spectacular sub-glacial meltwater channel of Cwm Gwaun, the frost-shattered rocks of Carningli and Carn Meini, and the deep valleys all around the Pembrokeshire coast which are "plugged" with glacial deposits and water-lain sands and gravels.

Not surprisingly, the vast range of environments crammed into this one small region makes it quite fascinating from the point of view of the wildlife enthusiast. Exposure is an important factor in determining the plant and animal species to be found in the different parts of Pembrokeshire, but the most important thing about the local climate is that it is *oceanic*. Naturally enough - for this is a lowland peninsula thrust westwards into the oceanic approaches of the British Isles - the climate is mild, equable and windy. There are frequent gales, and depressions carry moisture from the Atlantic Ocean far inland. Rainfall totals range from 30" or so at the coast to 60" or more in the Presely Hills. It seldom snows and in the coastal districts frosts are rare. Plant growth is therefore possible throughout the year, with summer growth favoured by the rarity of very high summer temperatures or periods of drought. The annual temperature range between the coldest month and the warmest month is only acout 12°C. Sunshine totals are high, especially in the coastal districts, and Dale is the sunniest place in Wales. As far as day-to-day weather is concerned, visitors will notice that Pembrokeshire is a *bracing* place, with bright clear light, sunny spells broken by short-lived cloudy episodes, and periods of rain that come and go so rapidly that umbrellas and bikinis are often needed on the same day!

Plants and Animals

Puffin

The vegetation of Pembrokeshire is, as might be expected, highly variable in composition and colour. Features that strike the visitor include the riot of colour as the spring and early summer flowers bloom in hedgerows and on coastal cliffs in May and June; the lush profusion of high summer vegetation in the inland areas; the effects of the wind in reducing tree growth in many of the exposed coastal districts and in creating grotesque wind-blown forms. Among the ubiquitous flowering plants are two species of gorse, which between them guarantee that vivid yellow gorse blossoms can be seen and smelt throughout the year. Inland there are snowdrops, primroses, bluebells, white and pink campions, celandines, buttercups, cow parsley and wild daffodils. Hedgerows are crowned with honeysuckle, blackthorn, hawthorn and bramble. On the coast we find sea campion, thrift, kidney vetch and vernal squill on the cliffs, and in the saltmarsh areas samphire, rice grass, sea lavender and sea purslane. Pembrokeshire woodlands are fascinating too, and the main decidious species (sycamore, alder, oak and ash) are widespread. The lower layers of the woodland canopy are often made up of hazel, elder, holly and blackthorn, with a tangle of ivy, honeysuckle and bramble in clearings and on the edges of dense woodland. There are many evergreens and conifers too, but the dense stands of spruce, larch and pine which now cover parts of Presely and parts of the lowlands too are lacking in the natural diversity of the native woodlands. The open moorlands, with their wide expanses of heather, bracken, tough grasses, mosses and rushes, are quite beautiful, especially in late summer and autumn when the heather is at its most colourful and when reds and browns spread across the landscape.

Pembrokeshire is an intensively-farmed region and even the moorlands of Presely are less wild than one might imagine. Habitats for large mammals are therefore somewhat restricted in extent. Nevertheless, badgers and foxes are common, and otters, polecats and mink are to be found in the remoter districts. The rabbit population is a sizeable one, but there are few hares. Grey squirrels, mice, rats and bats are common throughout the region. There are deer in some areas, and local naturalists suspect that muntjac deer exist in the fastnesses of Pembrokeshire woodlands. The largest local wild animals are the grey seals, which are common around the north coast.

Bird life is prolific in Pembrokeshire, particularly around the coast. The food resources of the sea, together with the abundance of safe nesting places on remote cliffs and on the Pembrokeshire islands, have encouraged the growth of a huge seabird population. Puffins, guillemots, razorbills, cormorants, gannets, shearwaters, kittiwakes, fulmar petrels - these and many other species are to be found nesting on the islands of Grassholm, Skomer, Skokholm and Ramsey. Numbers are difficult to calculate, but it is known, for example, that there are about 20,000 nesting pairs of gannets on Grassholm and 100,000 pairs of Manx shearwaters on Skomer. Visits to the islands are restricted by accessibility problems and by the requirements of nature conservation, but there are regular boat trips to both Skomer and Ramsey (see pages 36 and 38), and visits to the other "bird islands" can be arranged through the office of the

CARDS, GIFTS, NATURE TRAILS, BOOKS, INFORMATION ON VISITS TO SKOMER AND SKOKHOLM

Every purchase helps Wildlife. West Wales Trust for Nature Conservation

7 Market St., HAVERFORDWEST

Also seasonal Shops at Martins Haven; Brychan Yard, Upper Frog St., Tenby; and the Caravan at The Parrog, Newport.

West Wales Trust for Nature Conservation in Haverfordwest. Ring 0437-5462 for further information. If you are unable to visit the islands don't despair - nesting guillemots, razorbills and kittiwakes can be seen at Stack Rocks near Flimston, and puffins nest on Stackpole Head. On Dinas Head there are nesting cormorants and shags. Shelduck and other estuary birds nest in the Cleddau Wildfowl Sanctuary between Little Milford and Llangwm, and choughs, peregrines, herons, ravens and buzzards are among the scores of other birds to be found nesting around the coast. Favourite bird-watching sites include Bosherston Pools, Angle Bay, the Gann near Dale, St. David's Head, Strumble Head and the Nevern estuary at Newport. Inland Pembrokeshire has not suffered from hedge clearance on the scale of some other parts of Britain, so bird life is still relatively abundant even in the richest farming areas. Species like buzzard, magpie, heron, tawny owl, jay, pheasant, wood pigeon, great spotted woodpecker and mute swan are relatively abundant, and if you are lucky you will see kingfisher, barn owl, yellow wagtail, hoopoe and red kite. In all, 300 bird species have been recorded in Pembrokeshire, while over 100 species regularly breed here. Little wonder that the region is a naturalist's paradise ....

MUSIC CENTRE

Telephone: Haverfordwest 3261 or 2059

- Instruments and accessories
- Sheet music and books on music
- Records and cassettes

FOR THE BEST SELECTION

2-6 HIGH STREET
(AT THE TOP OF THE HILL BY THE CHURCH)

The fast, direct West Wales to Bristol express

HAVERFORDWEST—PEMBROKE—TENBY—CARMARTHEN—SWANSEA—CARDIFF—NEWPORT—BRISTOL

Connections at Haverfordwest for Littlehaven, Broadhaven, Dale and other beauty spots on the west coast.

For information concerning Haverfordwest/Tenby services, contact any South Wales Transport Office or National Express Agent. Tel: Swansea 475511 or Haverfordwest 3284.

FAST-DIRECT-RELIABLE

EXPRESSWEST

The National Park

The Pembrokeshire Coast National Park is neither as well-known nor as crowded as some of the other National Parks of Britain - but it is the only National Park that owes its existence primarily to the presence of magnificent and beautiful coast scenery. It was set up in 1952, with a designated area of 225 square miles, making it the smallest National Park in Britain. It is also unusual in that it is made up of four physically distinct segments, referred to generally by the NPA (the National Park Authority) as (a) the Southern Coast, (b) the Western and Northern Coasts, (c) the Presely Hills and North-East Coast, and (d) Daugleddau. These areas are shown on the location map on the back cover.

The South Coastal Area contains the most intensively-developed holiday resort complex of the National Park. The NPA finds it extremely difficult to control development in this area, with the result that caravan parks, guest houses, and new housing estates have spread across the countryside. Many people love the area; others hate it! Another feature of the south coastal zone is the presence of a military firing range inside the National Park boundary. This means that for much of the year, when firing and tank manoeuvres are in progress, the public is barred from large parts of the Castlemartin Peninsula and denied access to some of the most magnificent limestone cliff scenery in Western Europe. Even more grotesquely, we find that in the Angle Bay area the National Park contains much of the Texaco Oil Refinery, the old BP Ocean Terminal and the Kilpaison tank farm and pumping station. Foreign visitors will greet this news with amazement, dismay, or incredulity; but don't blame the officers of the NPA, since the responsibility lies fairly and squarely on the shoulders of the government for muddled priorities and muddled thinking. Should you start to feel depressed, just remember that the south coastal section of the National Park also contains glorious sandy beaches, havens of peace such as St. Govan's Chapel, Bosherston Pools, Caldey Island, Barafundle Bay and Stackpole Quay, and the wild and wide expanse of Freshwater West.

The Western and Northern Coasts are full of variety, and the area under the protection of the NPA includes the Dale Peninsula, the inner reaches of St. Bride's Bay, the greater part of the St. David's Peninsula, and most of Pen Caer. There is not so much holiday pressure on this area, although resort

Cerbid

Cottage Collection

SHEER LUXURY !!

QUALITY PERIOD COTTAGES

Enchanting warm Cottages of character and distinction in many beautiful parts of Wales. Some are on safe sandy beaches – others enjoy superb peaceful panoramic scenery. Highest domestic standards with Micro-waves, Dishwashers, Log Fires, Washing Machines and Colour T.V. Sleeping 2-14.

PETS WELCOME FREE

Very detailed Brochure from:
G.M. Rees, Cerbid Quality Cottages
Solva, Haverfordwest, Pembrokeshire
Telephone: (03483) 432/573

Wallis Woollen Mill weaves Design Centre Floor Rugs and fine washable Dress Fabrics, Tweeds and Flannels. Exclusive garment range. Educational Material. Small Tea Room.

Telephone: Clarbeston 297

Situated 8 miles NE of Haverfordwest, just off the B4329 Cardigan Road. Open: Mon. - Sat., 10 a.m. to 6 p.m. in Summer. No Coaches please.

settlements such as Dale, Little Haven and Broad Haven, Solva and St. David's are replete with visitors during the summer months. These settlements are really no larger than villages, and over long stretches of coastline the long-distance footpath walker encounters only the occasional cluster of cottages and the occasional clifftop farm. The beaches of these rough ocean coasts are well known for their golden sands and Atlantic breakers, and Whitesands Bay and Newgale Sands are popular with the surfboard fraternity. Broad Haven and Marloes Sands are other popular beaches, but for those who are happy without beach "facilities" there are scores of little sandy coves and creeks to be discovered. The cliffed coasts of the St. David's Peninsula are classed by earth scientists as among the most striking in the British Isles; there can be few more exhilarating walks than that between Newgale and Porth-clais or that between St. David's Head and Strumble Head.

The Presely Hills section of the National Park, which includes the coast between Fishguard and St. Dogmael's, is quite unique in character, combining fine, rolling upland scenery with rocky crags and deep wooded valleys. This is a truly Celtic landscape in which prehistoric features abound and in which the typical settlement pattern is one of scattered farmsteads and cottages and small loosely-knit hamlets. Newport is the only large settlement, with a population of just over 1,000! At Newport and Nevern Norman and later features can be seen cheek-by-jowl with very ancient Welsh landscape elements, and the rich mix of cultures and peoples is largely responsible for the magical and mystical atmosphere of this area. The coast has a character of its own too; Newport Bay has the finest beach on the north Pembrokeshire Coast, and the massive cliffs between Newport and Cemaes Head are in places more than 400 feet high. Mercifully, this whole area is free of industry and free of major holiday developments.

Daugleddau, referred to as the "inner sanctuary" of the National Park, is an area of beautiful river and pastoral landscape, with well wooded slopes and even fewer tourist developments than the Presely area. The pace of life here is slow and gentle, with rolling farmland in the Lawrenny-Landshipping area, extensive woodlands at Benton and Slebech Forest, and attractive park landscapes on the old estates of Picton and Slebech. But the focus of attention is the estuary itself, with the two Cleddau branches coming together at Picton Point, and then, downstream, side streams flowing into muddy "pills" or creeks and into the wide shallow estuaries of the Cresswell and Carew rivers. With every rise and fall of the tide this landscape (if such is the right word) transforms itself from pure waterway to

Longhouse, Abercastle (D. Beckwith).

Foel Drygarn summit, seen from Carn Alw

muddy estuary and back again. There are birds everywhere, their cries echoing around the steep wooded slopes that protect this special watery world from the sights and sounds of the busy world outside. It was not always so peaceful here; a century ago there were working coalmines on both sides of the estuary, coal barges and sailing ships in constant passage, limestone quarries working at West Williamston and Garron Pill, and at least half a dozen boat building yards on the stony river banks. Now most of the working vessels have gone, leaving fleets of pleasure craft in sole possession of the inner waterway.

It is not always appreciated that the Pembrokeshire Coast National Park is quite densely populated, with over 20,000 people living within its boundaries. Nearly all the land is privately owned, and local people have to try to make a living in ways that do not reduce the natural beauty or environmental value of the area. The NPA is not an autonomous body but a department of the County Council, receiving both local authority and government funding in order for it to carry out its objectives. These are the preservation and enhancement of natural beauty; the provision of opportunities for public enjoyment; the protection of the Park's distinctive wildlife and scientific and historic features; and the protection of the best interests of local people. The most contentious of the NPA's duties is in the field of planning and development control, and some local people feel that their economic and social welfare is treated as the lowest possible priority when planning decisions are being made. These criticisms may or may not be justified; but it is certainly true that the NPA has an exceedingly difficult task in balancing local needs against its statutory duty of environmental stewardship in the national interest. In the field of management and information services few would dispute that the NPA has an excellent record. Through its information centres, its walks and talks programmes, its publications, and its maintenance of footpaths, historic buildings and other public places the NPA is helping both local people and visitors to understand (and indeed *cherish*) the unique character of the region.

DID YOU KNOW . . .

that John Wesley visited Pembrokeshire on no less than 14 different occasions during his ministry?

that two breeds of dog, the Pembrokeshire corgi and the Sealyham terrier, originated in Pembrokeshire?

that one night in 1853 Mr. John Meyler of Cilciffeth and Mr. James Morris of Penbanc, not far from Fishguard, watched a phantom battle in the sky that lasted for about two hours?

that in the great basin called Cwm Cerwyn, on the south side of the Presely Hills ridge, King Arthur and his knights fought a pitched battle with the legendary wild boar called Twrch Trwyth?

that the Teifi Valley was the last haunt of the beaver in England and Wales?

that in the 1860's there was a serious plan to build a railway from Johnston to Broad Haven and thence to St. Davids?

that the slates used in the roof of the Palace of Westminster came from the Gilfach Quarry near Crymych?

that Bartholomew Roberts (known as "Black Bart"), one of the most notorious pirates of the eighteenth century, was born in the village of Little Newcastle in 1682?

that St. Govan's chapel, on the south Pembrokeshire coast, may have been the hermit's cell of Sir Gawaine, one of the knights of the Round Table?

that a dragon-embossed tablet found on the beach of Freshwater West is the only Viking artifact ever found in Pembrokeshire?

WOLFSCASTLE COUNTRY HOTEL AND RESTAURANT

Telephone: Treffgarne 225

Recommended by Egon Ronay, Michelin, A.A. Two Knives and Forks, B.T.A. Commended and other leading Guides

A la Carte and Table d'hôte Dinners
Interesting Bar Meals – Sunday Lunch
Tennis and Squash Courts
All Bedrooms with private facilities.
Equal distance between Fishguard and Haverfordwest, just off the main A40.

Open 7 days a week. Try us for good food.

RHOS DDU

OPEN FARM & NATURE TRAIL

CRYMYCH

Enjoy a super woodland walk by cottage ruins, stream and badger setts

FEED FARM ANIMALS AT 3.00 p.m.

HELP MILK THE HERD OF COWS AT 4.00 p.m.

Light Refreshments available

Indoor and Outdoor Picnic Area

OPEN:
JULY and AUGUST 10 a.m. to 6 p.m.
THE REST OF THE YEAR
1 p.m. to 6 p.m.

TELEPHONE JOYCE ON CRYMYCH 220

WINGANNA NATURAL FLEECES

Machine washable – Warm in winter – Cool in summer

For Babies as used in Cambridge University Research and seen on BBC TV Tomorrow's World
For over 17 years contented babies have slept on
Winganna Natural Lambswool Fleeces in the UK.

For Adults superb in the relief of backache in pregnancy.
Also recommended for insomnia, arthritis, back problems, etc.

Wertun Lambskin Chill Cheaters (Handmade Body Warmers).

STOP THE COLD DEAD!
Available for 1 year old through to adults
Access, Eurocard, Mastercard, Visa welcome.

WINGANNA NATURAL PRODUCTS, WINGANNA BARN, ST. ISHMAELS
HAVERFORDWEST, DYFED. TELEPHONE: DALE (06465) 403

A natural remedy for restless nights

Castle Square, Haverfordwest

INTRODUCING REAL FLOTILLA SAILING HOLIDAYS TO THE U.K.

Share a week of excitement with your family or friends on a flotilla holiday off the S.W. Coast of Wales.

As part of a group led by an experienced skipper you'll explore 24 miles of beautiful, sheltered estuary and the wild splendour of Pembrokeshire's Coastal National Park in a comfortable, robust, 28 foot, 6 berth sailing cruiser.

The action-packed itinerary includes windsurfing, water-skiing and dinghy sailing.

Discover your sense of adventure and phone or write for more details to:

Westfleet, Neyland Marina, Neyland, Milford Haven, Pembrokeshire. Telephone: (0554) 890627 or (0646) 601601.

Grey seals

The Islands

The Pembrokeshire islands have a magic of their own, and although they are not far offshore they are (with the exception of Caldey) uninhabited and wild, cherished nowadays as wildlife sanctuaries. All the islands are accessible given the right conditions of weather and tides, but there are dangerous tidal races in Ramsey Sound and Jack Sound, and Grassholm cannot be approached with safety when there is a swell or wind from the S or SW. All the main islands, apart from Caldey, are protected as nature reserves, and public access is strictly controlled. The notes below contain further information on landing procedures and boat schedules.

Caldey (Ynys Pyr) (140965)

The island is about 2 miles south of Tenby and about 600 acres in extent. It is made of limestone in the north and Old Red Sandstone in the south, rising to a maximum altitude of about 180 ft. Nowadays the island belongs to the monks of the Cistercian Order, and their Abbey is the most interesting of the inhabited buildings. The monks are farmers too, cultivating about 350 acres and giving the island a gentler and more productive appearance than the other islands. Since 1953 the monks have produced perfume from the gorse and lavender that grow in profusion. The island has some of the most interesting prehistoric cave sites in Pembrokeshire, and the bones of many Ice Age animals have been collected for display in Tenby Museum. The Celtic missionary St. Pyro (who is commemorated in the island's Welsh name) came here in the 6th century, and his community was the forerunner of a succession of religious communities over the centuries. The old priory and St. Illtud's Church were probably built around 1113 by Benedictine monks from St. Dogmael's, and they remained in occupation of the island until the dissolution of the monasteries in 1534. The parish church of St. David is an interesting primitive building, probably dating from the 6th century. After centuries of neglect the priory and two churches were restored around 1900 by the Rev. W. Done Bushell, and in 1912 the present Romanesque monastery was built by a small community of Anglican Benedictines. When the Benedictines moved to Prinknash in 1928, monks of the Cistercian Trappist order from Chimay in Belgium came in to replace them. Their small community remains in residence to this day.

With its lush vegetation (unusual for Pembrokeshire islands), its white-walled, red-roofed and pinnacled monastery, and its lovely flower gardens, Caldey has a Mediterranean feel about it. A number of families live on the island, and during the summer the population is swelled by up to 2,000 day visitors who enjoy the antiquities around the hamlet and the monastery, the magnificent cliff scenery and lovely beaches of Sandtop Bay, Priory Bay and Drinkim Bay. On the south-western cliffs there are thousands of sea-birds too. There are frequent boat trips to (and around) Caldey during the summer season; most departures are from Tenby Harbour. There are no landings on Saturdays and Sundays. Prices and sailing schedules from the kiosk on the harbour approach road.

Grassholm (598093)

Located about 7 miles west of Skomer, this little island is an RSPB reserve. It is the only gannetry in England and Wales, supporting about 20,000 breeding pairs of these magnificent birds. Other breeding birds include kittiwakes, shags, guillemots and razorbills. Puffins, which were once present in large numbers, now have only a small colony. The island is waterless, but green with fescue and other grasses except around the gannetry, where nests of dead grass and seaweed are closely packed. During the breeding season, especially when the young birds are being reared, the smell from the island is somewhat overpowering. There is no proper harbour, and landing can only be attempted in very calm weather.
For landing and round trips ring Dale Sailing Co. on Dale 349. There are also National Park Evening Cruises around the island; ring 0834-812175 for information.

Skomer (725094)

Like Caldey, Ramsey and Skokholm, the island has a Norse name, given to it by Viking sea-rovers in the ninth or tenth century A.D. Skomer is basically a detached segment of the Pembrokeshire coastal platform, about 722 acres in extent and made largely of volcanic rocks of Silurian age. It rises to a gentle summit 260 ft above sea-level. The faults and fractures in the rock have been picked out by the Atlantic breakers to create varied and spectacular cliff scenery, with deep steep-sided inlets cutting in towards the heart of the island. The soil (composed partly of glacial deposits left by the wasting Irish Sea Glacier about 14,000 years ago) is ideal for burrowing animals; puffins and Manx shearwaters have combined to create labyrinths of holes and tunnels which can all too easily be collapsed by unwary and clumsy visitors.

VISIT THE ISLANDS
DALE PRINCESS
BOAT TRIPS
Skomer: Landings and Round Skomer Cruises
Grassholm: Landings, Round and Evening Trips
All sailings depart Martin's Haven
DALE SAILING CO. LTD.
Tel: Dale 349
or any Information Centre

Puffins on Skomer Island

The island has a long history of settlement. There are old field enclosures and hut circles which probably date from Iron Age times, and during the Early Christian era there may have been a sizeable farming community here. After the Norman invasion the island was abandoned, although it continued to be used for the summer grazing of sheep and cattle and for rabbit-catching. About 3,000 were caught each year, and there was also a rich harvest of sea-birds and their eggs. In the 18th century a large farmhouse was built in the middle of the island, and from then until 1954 it was farmed more or less continuously, with cattle, sheep and pigs and good harvests of corn. Now it is abandoned, although a resident warden (who lives in a simple house near North Haven) looks after the island for the West Wales Trust for Nature Conservation during all but the winter months. The island is now a National Nature Reserve owned by the Nature Conservancy Council and managed by WWTNC. There are few trees, but the sheets of flowers which cover parts of the plateau and cliff tops during the early summer are among the glories of Pembrokeshire. There is also a rich marine life in the waters around the island, now protected by a Marine Reserve designation. This is one of Europe's finest sea-bird islands; in May and June visitors can see puffins, guillemots, razorbills, kittiwakes, shags, fulmars, and great and lesser black-backed gulls nesting in distinct colonies. The gull population has to be carefully controlled. Other nesting species include buzzards, ravens, choughs and short-eared owls. There are about 100,000 pairs of Manx

shearwaters on the island. They remain underground during the day, but at night the island is alive with their sounds, providing visitors with an unforgettable (if somewhat eerie!) experience.
Simple accommodation is available on the island for members of WWTNC for short stays only. Day visitors are welcomed on the island.
No dogs are allowed, and visitors are asked to keep to marked paths in order to minimise ecological damage. There are no toilets or other facilities. The Skomer boat leaves from Martin's Haven at regular intervals every day - weather permitting. Further information from Dale Sailing Co. on Dale 349, or from Tourist Information Centres.

Skokholm (735050)

This island is much smaller than Skomer, being only 240 acres in extent. It is made of Old Red Sandstone, and like Skomer it is a gently undulating platform bonded by steep cliffs. Again, there are hardly any trees. In the Middle Ages the island was used as a rabbit warren, and the seabirds also provided a rich harvest. Since the 18th century the island has been owned by the Dale Castle Estate. The farm buildings date from the 1700's and the only period of intensive farming occurred during the 1800's; but in spite of liming the soil proved too poor for survival, and the last farmer left in 1912. The island was popularised through the writings of R.M. Lockley, who leased Skokholm in 1927 and lived here unitl the onset of the Second World War. He kept some sheep, but his studies of sea-birds stimulated the creation of the Skokholm Nature Reserve, and between 1933 and 1976 it was run as a Bird Observatory, with many ornithological projects completed by research workers. Also, there was a comprehensive bird-ringing programme. Nowadays the island is leased by the WWTNC, and a resident warden keeps an eye on the bird colonies (mainly shearwaters, puffins, storm petrels, guillemots, razorbills, gulls and shags) between April and October. Day trips to the island are not allowed, but up to 15 visitors at a time can stay at the old farm. Weekend visits are organized during June and July. The WWTNC also organizes week-long courses (weather permitting!) on ornithology, photography and ecology; details can be obtained by ringing Haverfordwest 5462. Boat departures for round trips and landings are from Martin's Haven.

Gannets nest on Grassholm

Ramsey (Ynys Dewi) (705240)

Ramsey is separated from the south-western tip of the St. David's Peninsula by the treacherous waters of Ramsey Sound with a tidal race which at times reaches 15 knots. It is a hilly, rough island with a look of north Pembrokeshire about it; the rocky summits of Carn Llundain (446 ft) and Carn Ysgubor (323 ft) are reminiscent of Carnllidi and Penbiri on the mainland. There are prehistoric burial chambers on the hill summits. The island has a long religious history, and there were at one time two chapels - one dedicated to St. Justinian (St. David's confessor, who lived on the island) and the other to St. Dyfanog (who was one of the earliest Celtic missionaries in Britain, about 186 A.D.). For many centuries the island belonged to the Bishops of St. David's, and it was farmed and stocked with sheep and cattle. It produced good corn crops too. In the 1890's there was a corn-mill here, operated by a 14 ft water wheel. However, over the years farming became more and more difficult as rabbits became a plague and as isolation from the mainland added to the costs of living. A succession of owners and tenants have tried to make ends meet on the island, and it is now used for the raising of sheep and red deer. The island is still inhabited, and there is a bungalow available for overnight accommodation.

While the wildlife is not as prolific as that of Skomer, Ramsey is famous for its large colony of grey seals and as a breeding ground for chough and peregrine. Among the birds that breed on the island are guillemots, razorbills, fulmars, kittiwakes, and buzzards and ravens are always to be seen. A wonderful day may be had here, following the paths of the wild red deer to the magnificent viewpoints and stunning cliff scenery. There is a regular ferry landing visitors on all days except Saturdays. The first boat leaves St. Justinians at 9 a.m. Further information from St. Davids 720648 or 720662; or from the Tourist Information Centre or Ramsey Island Shop, both in the centre of St. Davids.

THE RAMSEY ISLAND SHOP

For the holiday souvenir that will always give pleasure come to The Ramsey Island Shop, the largest stockist of antiquarian maps and prints in Wales.

Take home an engraving of the places you have visited or an original print of the birds and flowers you have seen. We also have a wide selection of maps of Pembrokeshire and Wales from £5.00 - £1500.00. We guarantee that all our stock is genuine, since we sell no reproductions.

The Ramsey Island Shop
High Street, St. Davids
Telephone: St. Davids 720648

VISIT RAMSEY ISLAND

Experience the rugged unspoilt beauty of one of the UK's most spectacular islands, with its wild scenery and breathtaking views. You can see at close hand the large breeding colony of grey seals and the myriad of cliff-nesting sea birds. You are likely to see the peregrine and the chough and can be sure of watching the magnificent herd of wild red deer.

There is a regular ferry to and from the island every day except Saturday. The first boat leaves St. Justinians at 9 a.m.

Return Fare: Adults £2.50; Child £1.50
Landing Fee: £1.00 per person.

There are light refreshments and toilet facilities on the island. Dogs allowed with prior permission (ask at St. Justinians). All boats available subject to weather and sea conditions.

For further information and details of evening trips round the island contact The Ramsey Island Shop, High Street, St. Davids. Tel: 720648/720662

Situated on the Haverfordwest to St. David's Road (A487) at Simpson Cross. Drive straight into our Car Park from the main road!

We make everything from egg cups to complete dinner services and we are especially well known for our hand cut table lamps and hand decorated plant pot holders. Dragons galore! In fact, this is the home of the "character" dragon!

Commissions undertaken; all major credit cards accepted; mail order service. Visitors can see workshop "action" and are always welcome.

Telephone: Camrose (0437) 710628

THE PEMBROKESHIRE POTATO MARKETING GROUP LIMITED

Haverfordwest 2617

Puffin New Potatoes, please!

Ask your Greengrocer for them.

DID YOU KNOW …

that unil the early 1800's the village of St. Florence was accessible from the sea, with the lower part of the Ritec valley a tidal estuary?

that the monastery and settlement of St. David's were sacked and burnt on no less than eight occasions by the Vikings between 844 and 1091AD?

that the Milford Haven oil installations, when working at full capacity, eject over 1,000 tons of poisonous sulphur dioxide into the atmosphere every day?

that the red squirrel is now almost extinct in Pembrokeshire, having been displaced by the grey squirrel since it arrived in 1948?

that there are at least 20 Viking place-names in Pembrokeshire, including Fishguard, Ramsey, Skomer, Skokholm, Haverfordwest and Caldey?

that the Normans built more than 50 castles in Pembrokeshire, of which 15 were stone fortresses?

that during the Second World War there were no less than twelve operational air fields in Pembrokeshire?

that in the later part of the last century locally-mined coal was loaded onto sailing vessels at low tide on the sandy beaches of Little Haven, Nolton and Newgale?

that in Elizabethan times the local gentry hunted "wild" oxen in the Presely Hills?

that in 930AD Whitland Abbey was the setting for a great Assembly, convened by King Hywel Dda, at which Wales' first unified legal code was adopted?

Herring Gulls and their chicks on a Pembrokeshire cliff.

St. Margaret's Island (120793)

Located off the western tip of Caldey, this little island is about 14 acres in extent. There was originally a causeway connecting it with Caldey, and it is still possible (but dangerous!) to scramble across from one island to another at low tide. In Norman times there was a monastic cell here, and some of the ancient buildings were later used by quarrymen during limestone quarrying operations. A century ago about 20 people lived on the island, even indulging in a little farming to help them survive. St. Margaret's has the largest cormorant colony in Wales - about 300 breeding pairs - and it is managed as a nature reserve by the West Wales Trust for Nature Conservation. Landing is prohibited except by prior arrangement.

Cardigan Island (160516)

This island of about 40 acres is less than a quarter of a mile offshore on the eastern side of the Teifi estuary. The surface is undulating and grassy, with sheets of bluebells in the spring. There are about 900 nesting pairs of herring gulls and numerous other birds, but the island's main claim to fame is that it has a small flock of Soay Sheep. The island has been a nature reserve since 1944, owned by the WWNT since 1963. There are nowadays no rats on the island (they were killed off in 1968) and there are hopes that Manx shearwaters and puffins can be induced to begin nesting here. Access is by permit only, and is in any case quite difficult. There are occasional boat trips round the island from St. Dogmael's.

Gateholm (770072)

A small island at the west end of Marloes Sands, Gateholm can be reached by a scramble across the rocks at low tide. It is about 20 acres in extent, well covered with thick grassy turf and bracken. The fascinating thing about this island is that it was once densely populated; there are over 100 hut circle foundations, probably dating from the Iron Age, and archaeological finds suggest later habitation too, probably during the Middle Ages. The settlement may have been a monastic community. Following the Norman conquest sheep were grazed on the island, and grazing has continued intermittently to this day.

Pembrokeshire Coastal Footpath in the early summer.

Below: Cliffs on Skomer Island.

The smaller Islands

In addition to the main islands mentioned above there are a number of rocks and skerries which deserve mention. *St. Catherine's Island*, **which can be reached across Tenby beach at low tide, supports a massive fort built between 1868 and 1875; it was planned as part of the defensive scheme for Milford Haven during the Napoleonic Wars. Other forts were built on** *Thorn Island* **(1852-59) and on** *Stack Rock* **(1859-67) inside the Milford Haven waterway. The former is now a hotel, relatively easy of access from West Angle Bay; the latter is seldom visited, and is still in a good state of repair. Some 20 miles out into the Atlantic, west of Grassholm, are** *The Smalls*. **These, together with other reefs called** *The Hats and Barrels*, **are extremely dangerous, being constantly swept by swells and storm waves. The first Smalls lighthouse was built in 1776 - a famous octagonal structure supported on stout timber legs. This light survived until 1852, and was then replaced by the present lighthouse. There is another lighthouse (built in 1839) on South Bishop Rock, the southernmost of the** *Bishops and Clerks* **to the west of Ramsey. These rocks and islets were also much feared by mariners, and there are many stories of shipwrecks, maroonings, and sea rescues asssociated with them. Puffins were once harvested from the larger rocks, and sheep were ferried out during the summer for grazing on them. The islands of** *Ynys Beri* **and** *Ynys Cantwr* **lie just off the southern tip of Ramsey and** *Midland Isle* **lies just off the eastern tip of Skomer. The latter is 21 acres in extent and was once used for grazing.**

FISHING & WALKING ENTHUSIASTS
THE LAST *"PINT AND MEAL"* BEFORE

LLYS-Y-FRAN DAM

(ONE OF PEMBROKESHIRE'S BEAUTY SPOTS-NOT TO BE MISSED)

THE

CROSS INN

CLARBESTON ROAD
Nr. HAVERFORDWEST

Telephone: Clarbeston 506

(only 5 miles - bear right off B4329 before Crundale)

Extensive Menu including Cold Table and Steaks etc.
Local Salmon (when available)
Beer Garden ● Real Ale ● Live Entertainment Fridays
Children Welcome
Parties and Weddings Catered for

LLEITHYR FARM MUSEUM

Near Whitesands Bay, St. David's

Telephone: 0437 - 720245

DISPLAYS OF

- ★ Agricultural Implements
- ★ Tractors
- ★ Farm Carts
- ★ Dairy Utensils
- ★ Tools
- ★ Domestic Bygones
- ★ Video Theatre
- ★ Gift Shop

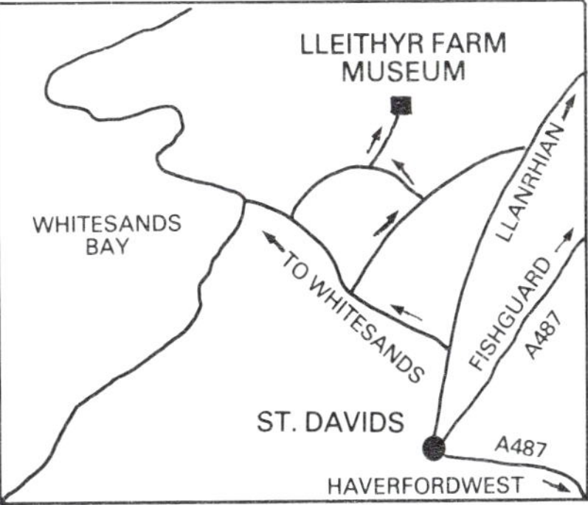

Limited Opening during April

Open Daily
MAY - OCTOBER
10 a.m. - 5 p.m.
(Closed Mondays except Bank Holidays)

National Park Award Winner 1985

Manorbier Castle, as it appeared a century ago

Pre-History and History

There are literally hundreds of fascinating cultural monuments to be visited in Pembrokeshire. The greatest problem for the visitor is how to pick and choose those cromlechs, Iron Age forts, churches and castles, mansions and domestic buildings which will prove most interesting. The Gazetteer on pages 88-106 of this Guide contains much information which will be of use, but to set the scene the following paragraphs explain in simple terms the main phases in the settlement of the area, listing just a small selection of "top historical sites".

Stone Age: People have lived in Pembrokeshire for 20,000 years or more. The earliest inhabitants were the Palaeolithic hunters who lived in caves such as Cat's Hole (Monkton), Hoyle's Mouth (Penally), and various caves on Caldey Island. The Middle Stone Age peoples were more skilled in the making of tools and weapons, and they survived by hunting, fishing and the gathering of nuts, berries and edible plants in various coastal areas which are now submerged beneath sea-level. The people of the New Stone Age (Neolithic) period were the first farmers; they migrated into Pembrokeshire by sea, and we are reminded of their existence by the great chambered tombs which they built of boulders and covered with earth mounds or barrows. The cromlechs at Pentre Ifan (099370), Longhouse (848335), Trellyffant (082425), Burton (972082) and Carreg Coetan (Newport) (059393) are splendid examples of these chambered tombs, still impressive even though their covering barrows have been stripped away by the passage of time.

Bronze Age: The Beaker people of the Bronze Age spread far and wide over the Pembrokeshire landscape, bringing with them pottery-making and metal-working skills. They cremated their dead, placing the ashes in pottery containers which were then covered with round barrows or cairns. These round barrows or "tumuli" are found all over Pembrokeshire, for example at Plumstone Rock (917234), on the summit of Foeldrygarn (158336), at Crugiau Cemais (125416) not far from Moylgrove, and at Dry Burrows (948997) on the South Pembrokeshire Ridgeway. Bronze Age people also erected standing stones, for example at Bedd Morris (038365), Mabesgate (828076) and Rhos y Clegyrn (913355), and were responsible for stone circles and stone alignments, most of which have been destroyed. The only stone circle

DID YOU KNOW ...

that considerable damage was done to St. David's Cathedral in the year 1248 by an earthquake which was widely felt throughout southern Britain?

Pentre Ifan Cromlech

CASTELL HENLLYS

Heneb/Ancient Monument

Iron Age Fort/Romano-British Annexe (off A487 Cardigan-Fishguard)

Reconstructions, excavations, crafts, herbs and crops

Celtic Feasts in July and August

Open over Easter and in May, July, August, September

Set in beautiful Pembrokeshire National Park – an historic day out, explained for all ages to enjoy. Picnic area, Shop, Warriors' Training Course. Telephone: Crosswell 319

Castell Henllys Iron Age round house

worthy of note is at Gors Fawr near Mynachlogddu (135294), while the best stone alignment, called Parc-y-Meirw (The Field of the Dead), is located at 998359 on the mountainside above Llanychaer. A good example of a massive pair of stones (one male and the other female?) is at Cerrig Meibion Arthur (118310) in the great basin of Cwm Cerwyn beneath the Presely summit.

Iron Age: About 2,500 years ago Iron Age immigrants of Celtic stock began to arrive in Pembrokeshire, and their structures dominate the prehistoric landscape. Their "raths" can be seen all over the map of Pembrokeshire. Mostly these are small promontory forts (around the coast) or hill-forts inland. The settlers often used river spurs for their defended settlement sites where there were no high hills available, as at Castell Henllys (118390), where a replica Iron Age round house has been constructed and opened to the public. Good examples of coastal promontory forts can be seen at Greenala Point (007966), Flimston Castles (930945), Great Castle Head (798156) and at Marloes Deer Park (758090). On St. David's Head (722279) there is a large camp contained within the stone-built defences of the Warrior's Dyke, with other stone defences further east and a pattern of stone-walled Iron Age fields in the Porthmelgan valley. There are three magnificent hill forts in Pembrokeshire - on the summits of Foeldrygarn (157336), Carningli (062372), and Garn Fawr (895388). All three have stone walls and ditches on an impressive scale, with traces of hut circles and enclosures inside the fortifications and stone-walled fields outside. Some of these features, and indeed many of the features of the smaller promontory and inland forts all over Pembrokeshire, may date from the time of Christ or even later. Indeed, the best-defended sites may well have remained in use up to the time of the Norman Conquest.

The Age of the Saints: Following the breakup of the Roman Empire there was a great revival of Celtic culture, and there was much immigration into Pembrokeshire from Ireland. Settlements from this time may well have been established at such coastal sites as Gateholm (768071) and Sheep Island (843016) and at Clegyr Boia (737251) near St. David's. Many of the settlements were connected with the missionary activities of the Celtic saints; sometimes these started off as isolated religious cells, while others were larger religious communities. St. David's, St. Dogmael's, Nevern, Penally and Caldey were all important centres at this time. Probably many of the churches built in Norman times and rebuilt in the 1800's are on the sites of little wooden churches constructed in the fifth and sixth centuries A.D. There are few buildings dating from this time, but the main traces of the Age of the Saints are to be found in the wonderful Celtic Crosses and inscribed stones. Most of the earlier inscribed stones are to be found in the Gwaun Valley, in Nevern and St. David's, while the later great Celtic Crosses (of which only three survive) are at Nevern, Penally and Carew. There are also many stones which have inscriptions written in the strange Ogam alphabet, which originated in Ireland.

Pentre Ifan Burial Chamber

The *cromlech* or dolmen at Pentre Ifan (SN 099370) is one of the most imposing prehistoric monuments in the whole of Wales. It is beautifully situated on the flank of a ridge overlooking the Nevern Valley, with the rocky crag of Carningli dominating the landscape to the west. The monument as we see it today consists of a group of tall pillars, three of which support a massive capstone measuring almost 17 feet long by 10 feet wide. The base of the capstone is about 7'6'' above the ground, and it is said to weigh over 16 tons. Beneath this capstone was the actual chamber used by the Neolithic people for the burial of their dead, but when the structure was built about 4,500 years ago it looked quite different. At that time the *cromlech* was completely buried beneath an elongated barrow or mound about 120 ft long and some 60 ft wide. The mound was aligned more or less north-south, and it must have risen to a height of at least 10-12 feet above the present ground surface at its southern end. This is the end where the chamber and crescent-shaped facade or portal of standing stones were located. The burial chamber was excavated in 1936-37 and again in 1958-59, and it is the most frequently-visited of all the megalithic monuments in Pembrokeshire.

St. David (Dewi Sant)

Much of the life of Dewi Sant, the patron saint of Wales, is shrouded in mystery. As with all saints, it is difficult to separate fact from legend when we read history, but there can be no doubt that Dewi was a real figure who lived in the sixth century and who inspired the faithful both in this little corner of Pembrokeshire and further afield. Dewi was born to Non, the daughter of a local chieftain, on the site of St. Non's Chapel overlooking the waters of St. Bride's Bay. He was trained as a priest near Aberaeron and later in the monastery of Ty Gwyn, near the present city which bears his name. His missionary life was spent for the most part far away in other parts of the Celtic world, but he returned to his home district to establish his monastery, and in his old age he was visited by disciples and students from as far afield as Brittany, Cornwall and Ireland. He travelled to Rome and Jerusalem and returned as archbishop. Having spread his reputation as a theologian and Man of God over a wide are, he died on 1st March in the year 588. The influence of his ministry was so great that more than 50 medieval churches were established in his name. Dewi was canonized in 1120, and he is now the patron saint of Wales.

For hardy Nursery Stock
visit
NEVERN NURSERIES
(E. Leah)
Nevern, near Newport
Tel: Newport 820330
Coastal and unusual Shrubs
Our Speciality

CHRISTIAN BOOKSHOP
25 Market Courtyard
Haverfordwest
Books - Cards
Stationery - Tapes
Handmade Crafts
by Tearcraft

The Norman Conquest: When the Normans arrived in Pembrokeshire in 1053 they transformed both the local way of life and the local landscape. They established themselves firmly in the south of the county, driving out or absorbing the members of the Welsh-speaking community and creating what was later to be called "Little England Beyond Wales". They built many stockaded earthworks to defend their colony, later to be replaced by motte and bailey castles and then by the mighty stone fortresses which are so characteristic of the Pembrokeshire scene today. Their main fortresses were at Pembroke and Haverfordwest, and a "line" of castles across the county (at Roch, Wiston, Llawhaden, Narberth and Amroth) lay a little way south of the high water mark of Norman settlement in mid-Pembrokeshire. Although there was never a truly fortified frontier here, the line eventually crystallised out as The Pembrokeshire Landsker, separating a Welsh-speaking community in the north from an English-speaking community in the south. The Landsker survives to this day. Inside the Englishry the Normans built other castles at Tenby, Manorbier, Picton and Carew, with large fortified manor houses at Dale, Angle, Eastington (901025), Upton, Benton and Bonville's Court near Saundersfoot. They also built splendid bishop's palaces at St. David's and Lamphey. Inside the Welshry the Normans built stone castles at Newport, Cardigan and Cilgerran. In addition to the castles which are so popular with tourists nowadays there are more than 30 "forgotten" castles - fortified mounds built by the Welsh princes during their campaigns against the Norman invaders, short-lived Norman motte and bailey castles, and old fortified manor houses. They are dotted all over Pembrokeshire, and nowadays appear simply as overgrown mounds with surrounding ditches full of brambles. Why not hunt for some of them? An excellent map of their locations is to be found in the booklet *Castles of Pembrokeshire* by Dillwyn Miles. The influence of the Normans and their followers on church architecture is striking. The great cathedral at St. David's owes its present form above all else to the building skills and ambitions of the Norman bishops in the four centuries after 1180. The religious houses of St. Dogmael's Abbey, Pill Priory (Milford), Haverfordwest Priory and Friary, Monkton Priory and Caldey Priory were all built in the centuries following the Norman Conquest. The large churches dedicated to St. Mary in Haverfordwest, Pembroke and Tenby (all three in Norman walled towns) are magnificent, and like many of the other parish churches of south Pembrokeshire they have tall, solid towers. These towers, often castellated and with slit windows, are among

Hermitage Antiquities

Fine Quality Arms, Armour and Militaria for the Collector. Specialists in 16th and 17th Century items.

Weapons bought, sold and exchanged.

FISHGUARD
10 West Street.
Telephone: 873037 & 872322

the diagnostic features of the Anglo-Norman colony; see them, for example, at Gumfreston, Begelly, Llanstadwell, Castlemartin, Carew Cheriton and Steynton. In contrast the churches of the Welshry are smaller, often located in isolated places and built with simple bellcotes rather than towers. Examples can be seen at Llanwnda, Llysyfran, Spittal and Roch.

Among the other traces left by the Normans in the landscape are the hundred or so "new" villages created with the establishment of manors and the immigration of settlers from Flanders, Devon and Cornwall, Hereford and Gloucester. These villages usually have English-sounding names - as at Hodgeston, Jeffreyston, Reynalton, Jameston and East Williamston. Some of these memorial settlements were located well to the north of the present-day Landsker, at Henry's Moat, New Moat, Puncheston, Ambleston and Letterston; some of these have declined almost the status of "deserted villages".

Some of the Norman villages in Pembrokeshire have the classic features normally associated with English villages - village green, village pond, church, rectory, manor-house and castle mound all clustered together with farms and cottages. This nucleated type of village was, and still is, foreign to the Welsh tradition, for Welsh communities have always been loosely-knit ones, with cottages and farms dotted about the landscape in a somewhat haphazard way.

In parts of Pembrokeshire it is also still possible to see another trace of the Norman world - namely the strip fields (made from the old open fields of the feudal system) still to be found in villages like Cosheston, Angle and Letterston.

Flemish Chimneys

At one time there were many farmhouses with round chimneys in Pembrokeshire. Few of these now remain, although good examples can be seen in the St. David's area and in the village of St. Florence near Tenby. Traditionally the chimneys are referred to as "Flemish chimneys", but they don't actually seem to have had anything to do with Flanders or with the Flemish immigrants who came to Pembrokeshire in the twelfth century. Most of the buildings which have these chimneys were built in the fifteenth and sixteenth centuries as houses for yeoman farmers, and it is now believed that the builders were simply using techniques developed and then handed down during the period of castle-building in Pembrokeshire. Arched doorways, stone staircases, stone benches and massive stone walls with slit windows are other features which can be seen both in domestic architecture and also in more imposing buildings such as Pembroke Castle and the Bishop's Palace at St. David's.

Manorbier Castle interior

Newport Castle, now used as a residence

ROBESTON HOUSE HOTEL

A Georgian Manor House set in 5½ acres on the main A40 road at Robeston Wathen.

Open all year

All bedrooms en-suite with tea and coffee making facilities and colour T.V.

Restaurant open to non-residents. A la carte and Country House menus. Licensed Bar.

Morning coffee, light lunches and afternoon teas.

Mini-breaks available.

Ideal venue for touring Pembrokeshire and for country holidays - shooting, fishing and riding available.

Telephone: Narberth (0834) 860392

MAESLLYN MILL

(Near Llandysul)

- ★ Woollen Weaving
- ★ Museum
- ★ Spinning Classes
- ★ Shop
- ★ Coffee and Home Made Food
- ★ Nature Trail
- ★ Fishing

**WET OR FINE –
THE BEST DAY OUT
FOR ALL THE FAMILY**

Monday to Saturday 10 - 6.
Sunday 2 - 6.

Situated between Croeslan on the A486 and Penrhiwpal on the B4571.

Telephone: Rhydlewis 251

The Landsker

The Landsker is a mysterious (and invisible) line which runs across Pembrokeshire from Newgale on St. Bride's Bay to Amroth on Carmarthen Bay. Ever since the early Middle Ages it has divided the English of the south (the area known as "Little England") from the Welsh of the north. Originally, following the Norman Conquest, the Landsker marked quite a sharp frontier, for the Normans and their followers were bent upon setting up a strong and secure colony centred upon the great waterway of Milford Haven and protected by the castles of Pembroke and Haverfordwest and by a host of smaller fortresses. In the north the Welsh population (swelled by innumerable refugees from the south) contrived to carry on a more or less traditional way of life, but between 1100 and 1400 conflicts were frequent between the Normans and the Welsh Princes and even among the Welsh Princes themselves.

As late as 1600 the Landsker was so sharp in some places that George Owen, Pembrokeshire's Elizabethan chronicler, was able to describe places where Welsh-speaking people and English-speaking people were separated by no more than the width of a pathway. Now times have changed, but the Landsker can still be traced across the landscape and the two parts of Pembrokeshire still retain many of their ancient characteristics.

A number of the castles and other medieval buildings of Pembrokeshire are still inhabited ...

DID YOU KNOW ...

that the quiet hamlet of Landshipping, on the shore of the Daugleddau opposite Picton Ferry, was the scene of a great mining disaster which claimed the lives of more than 40 men and boys in 1844?

that in the early part of the last century there were at least three working windmills in Tenby?

that the world's first ironclad warship, the *Warrior*, launched in 1860, was for many years tied up at Pembroke Ferry and used as a floating jetty for a naval oil storage depot?

that some of the largest oil tankers visiting Milford Haven are a quarter of a mile long, so long that the members of the crew use bicycles to get from one end to the other?

CAMBRIAN INN

A group of "medieval" craft producers with their wares

Riverside Gallery

A lovely Shop by the River selling an unusual range of

QUALITY GIFTS AND CRAFTWORK

including Craft Jewellery, Pottery, Glass Engraving and many more items

"For a Gift that's different!"

17 RIVERSIDE ARCADE
HAVERFORDWEST

Telephone: Haverfordwest 4295

THE GOLDEN PLOVER ART GALLERY

**Warren, Pembroke
Pembrokeshire SA71 5HR**

Water colours of Pembrokeshire, Venice and other places abroad; relief constructions and fabric collages by BIM and ARTHUR GIARDELLI

The Gallery is next to the spectator area for the Castlemartin Ranges on the Warren to Castlemartin road. It is usually open but a telephone call would be appreciated.

Telephone: Castlemartin 201

Arts and Crafts

Pembrokeshire has produced few great artists, although the region's landscapes (especially around the coast) have provided inspiration for many artists of international repute. Among these we can number Turner, Wilson, Graham Sutherland, John Piper, Augustus John and Ceri Richards. Many have remarked on the special quality of Pembrokeshire light and on the vivid colourings to be found, especially in spring and early summer; many have returned to paint the same scene over and again in different light conditions. Just as Cornwall was a Mecca for artists in past decades, Pembrokeshire now has a sizeable artist community, and top-quality works can be seen and purchased in galleries all over the region. Some of these are listed below.

As far as craftsmanship is concerned, the Pembrokeshire tradition is for small-scale or cottage crafts. The only "industrialised" craft activity in the last century was the weaving of Welsh woollens, and of the hundreds of little woollen mills that were scattered around the steep-sided valleys of Pembrokeshire only 3 now remain. Until the 1960's there was a sharp decline in other craft activities also, with mass-produced goods taking the place of traditional hand-made items in homes and on farms. Now things have changed. Since Pembrokeshire became a popular tourist area many little craft workshops have been set up, producing well-made hand-crafted items for sale.

Art Galleries

Here are just a few, some providing a selection of local works for sale, and others mounting permanent or semi-permanent exhibitions.

Castle Museum and Art Gallery, Haverfordwest
David Tress Gallery, Horns Lane, Haverfordwest
County Library Exhibition Hall, Dew Street, Haverfordwest
The Coach House Gallery, The New Quay, Haverfordwest
Fron Farm Gallery, Llanycefn, Clynderwen
Graham Sutherland Gallery, Picton Castle
The Gallery (John Knapp-Fisher), Trevigan Cottage, Croesgoch
J.V. Reason Jones, Upper Frog Street, Tenby
John Rogers Gallery, Peter's Lane, St. David's
Rosedale Studio, West Street, Newport

Craft producers at Haverfordwest Medieval Craft Fayre

VISIT

CILGWYN CANDLES

WORKSHOP

AND

MINI-MUSEUM

Tenby Pottery, 14 Upper Frog Street, Tenby
Penally Pottery, Landsker House, Penally
Begelly Pottery, Begelly, near Kilgetty
Tuson Ceramics, The Pottery, Walwyn's Castle, near Haverfordwest
Honeyborough Pottery, Honeyborough Green, Neyland
Hafod Hill Pottery, Llanboidy, Whitland
Cecily Jellyman (creative embroidery), Rhosfach Farm Studio, Crosswell, near Crymych
Waterfall Knitwear, The Old Corn Mill, Ponthirwaun, Cardigan
Jean Wilks (ceramic beads), Porth-y-Castell, Cilgerran
Old Forge Crafts (lovespoons, model boats), Alltybont, Llanglydwen, Whitland
John Thomas (harp-maker), Sealyham Home Farm, Wolfscastle
Inwood, Cold Inn, Broadmoor, near Saundersfoot
E.B. Owen and Son (ornamental ironwork), Forgemill Works, Templeton
J.E. Thomas and Son (ornamental ironwork), Smithfield Forge, Dinas Cross, Newport
Arc-en-Ciel Knitwear Designs, Lampeter House, Lampeter Velfrey, Narberth
Laugharne Pottery, King Street, Laugharne
Paul Webb Pottery, Kiln Road, Haverfordwest
Marigold's Woolshed, Mynachlogddu, nr. Maenclochog
Julian King-Salter (pottery), Fachongle Isaf, Cilgwyn, Newport

PAUL WEBB POTTERY

at

8 Holloway & Kiln Rd.
Haverfordwest, Dyfed
(0437) 68279

Paul Webb makes a full range of hand thrown tableware in high-fired stoneware. He also specialises in exclusive commissioned pieces.

THE SMITHY CRAFTSHOP

Cenarth Falls
Newcastle Emlyn, Dyfed SA38 9JL

The Craftshop specialises in Celtic Jewellery, Local Pottery, Woodcarvings, Welsh Woollen Goods, Books and Glassware in addition to Basketware, Rural Victoriana and Antique Exhibits.
Situated on the A484.
Telephone: (0239) 710067

Pembrokeshire

CRAFT MARKETS

Organized by the local association of cottage craft producers

Many venues through the summer
See local press for details

Secretary: Norman Vessey
Telephone: Hebron 241

Marion Batt demonstrating the technique of spinning at a local craft market.

Woollen Mills

The woollen industry in Pembrokeshire has a very long history, and rough cloth was certainly being made before the arrival of the Normans in 1094. After 1300 the industry developed quickly, and the skills of Flemish immigrants helped to bring about greater production for sale and even export. Pembrokeshire cloth was very rough, and it was used only for the cheapest fabrics and for clothes for poorer people. In the 1500s and 1600s rough woollen cloth was exported from Tenby, Haverfordwest, Pembroke and other small ports. Early in the nineteenth century the invention of carding and spinning machinery and power looms led to the establishment of many small woollen factories in the deep valleys of Pembrokeshire where water power could be used. By 1850 there were hundreds of woollen mills and fulling mills in the county. In 1900 the number had fallen to about 25, but now only three of the old mills remain - at Wallis (Ambleston), Middle Mill (Solva) and Tregwynt (St. Nicholas). Althoughn these mills now use electrically-driven machinery, all three are well worth visiting.

Alan Hemmings handlooms his unique mohair and wool shawls, scarves, hats and cloaks on traditional wooden looms.

Craftsmens Gallery, Budget Shop and good coffee too!

EASTER TO CHRISTMAS: WEEKDAYS 10-5

Leave A478 Tenby/Cardigan road at Efailwen and aim for the Taf valley. 7 miles north of the A40 at Whitland via Henllan Amgoed and Cwm Miles.

STUDIO IN THE CHURCH

IN THE ANCIENT CHURCH OF CILMAENLLWYD

Nr. Login, Whitland, Dyfed.
Tel: Clynderwen (09912) 676

The Bishop's Palace in St. David's, a superb example of medieval craftsmanship in stone.

SILCOX COACHES

SILCOX GARAGE

What to do

For those who enjoy active holidays there are now excellent facilities for sport and recreation all over Pembrokeshire. The following list gives some indication of the opportunities that exist in various locations; for fuller information visitors are advised to acquire the Preseli DC *Holiday Activities* pack of leaflets and to enquire at tourist information centres.

Boat trips along the coast, to and from the islands, and within Milford Haven, are readily available. The following are the main departure points: St. Dogmael's, Cardigan, Newport, Lower Town Fishguard, St. Justinian's, Solva, Martin's Haven, Dale, Hobbs Point (Pembroke Dock), Tenby, Saundersfoot.

Sailing instruction is available at Fishguard, Dale, Llanstadwell, Neyland, Pembroke Dock, Tenby and Saundersfoot.

Boats for hire from Fishguard, Newport, Neyland, Nolton, Dale, Tenby, Saundersfoot. These boats include sailing boats, rowing dinghies and canoes.

Sub aqua. This activity is naturally carefully controlled. But there are a number of contacts for those who would like lessons or hired equipment. Main contact addresses - Tenby, Saundersfoot, Milford Haven, Neyland, Cardigan.

Wind surfing, surfing and canoeing are becoming increasingly popular. The main surf beaches are Whitesands, Newgale, Marloes and Freshwater West, but canoeing and wind surfing are now popular at many venues around the coast. Equipment can be hired from Whitesands Bay, Tenby and Saundersfoot.

Sea fishing is a popular pastime in beaches, estuaries and bays all round the Pembrokeshire coast; the main catches are mackerel, pollock, bass and flounders.

Boat fishing can be tried by the novice at little expense, since regular fishing trips now set off from the main centres such as St. Dogmael's, Newport, Fishguard, St. Justinian's, Solva, Dale, Neyland, Tenby and Saundersfoot. There are at least 20-30 vessels licensed for inshore fishing-trips. The main catches are mackerel, pollock, bass, ray, skate, and even tope and shark.

River and reservoir fishing. Fishing licenses and also permits are required. The main fishing rivers are the Teifi, Nevern, Eastern Cleddau and Western Cleddau. Brown trout are common, but salmon and also sewin (sea trout) are to be found in the main rivers. Permits and licenses for river fishing can be obtained at many tackle shops and other

A new residential outdoor centre in the heart of Pembrokeshire's National Park with adventure and excitment now available by the day.

Try these...abseiling, assault course, canoeing, climbing, coasteering, landyachting, pony trekking, sailing, the Twr-y-Felin Challenge (a chance to test your own 'Krypton Factor'), or take it easy on a guided coast walk.

Combine two or more to make an exciting multi-activity day. Prices from £1.50/Hr. to £16/Day. B & B/Full board for active people from £8.50 per night.

UNION SUNDOWN
S·U·R·F H·I·R·E

A wide range of high quality surfing equipment including malibu boards, windsurfers, boogie boards and wetsuits is available for hire by the hour, half day or day.

Windsurfing and surfing lessons are run every day, subject to prevailing wind and sea conditions.

Canoeing lessons take place every week, run by B.C.U. Senior Instructors. All standards are catered for and basic awards may be taken.

Prices from £1/Hr. to £17.50/3 Hrs.

TWR-Y-FELIN OUTDOOR CENTRE & UNION SUNDOWN
WEST WALES ADVENTURE SPECIALISTS
FOR FUN & ACTION, INFORMATION OR MORE PHONE: ST. DAVIDS 720391 (ANYTIME)

National Park walk - Presely Hills

addresses. There is reservoir fishing for brown and rainbow trout at Llysyfran and Rosebush; information from WWA. Coarse fishing in Bosherston Pools.

Horse riding and pony trekking are nowadays very popular holiday pastimes. The best trekking country is in the Presely Hills, but riding and pony centres are dotted all over Pembrokeshire. Some of the centres provide full accommodation and organize residential holidays. Others arrange day treks or shorter rides, charged by the hour. See the National Park *Riding and Pony Trekking* leaflet, which is particularly useful.

Golf. There are a number of fine courses in Pembrokeshire, some of them in spectacular coastal locations. The main ones are at Tenby (18 holes), Pembroke Dock (9 holes), Milford Haven (18 holes), Haverfordwest (18 holes), St. David's (9 holes), Newport (9 holes) and Cardigan (18 holes). Bar snacks and full meals are available at club-houses, and lessons can be arranged.

Squash. There are squash courts at Gwbert (Cardigan), Wolfscastle, Haverfordwest, Neyland, Bush (Pembroke Dock) and Wooden (Saundersfoot). Visitors are welcome to book in for games, but most courts are heavily booked by members.

Tennis. Public courts are available for hire at Newport, Dinas, Wolfscastle, Milford Haven, Haverfordwest, Pembroke Dock, Tenby and Saundersfoot.

Bowls. Greens are available to the public (when there are no matches in progress) at Milford Haven, Haverfordwest, Fishguard, Pembroke Dock, Tenby and Saundersfoot.

Swimming Pools are available at Cardigan, Crymych, Haverfordwest, Milford Haven, Pembroke Dock and Tenby.

Other Sports include badminton, field archery, rock climbing, land yachting, para-scending and water-skiing. Contact the tourist information centres for details.

Visit
Y Felin

Llangloffan
FARM

The Teifi Coracle

The coracle is an immensely ancient craft which may well have been used by the Iron Age immigrants who came to Pembrokeshire. Its construction has changed hardly at all over two thousand years, and each of the West Wales rivers had its own particular coracle type. The Teifi coracle has to cope with fierce eddies and it is made to sit deeper in the water than the Tywi coracle. It also has a "pinched-in" waist where the seat is located amidships. The vessel, which is strictly a one-man craft, is made of a frame of laths of willow and hazel covered with a calico skin which is stitched on and treated with pitch and linseed oil for waterproofing. The coracle has to be light enough for one man to carry.

A century ago there were more than 300 coracles on the Teifi alone. Now there are only a handful left.

Last Week in May

Famous international Artists performing in one of Britain's loveliest Cathedrals.

Details from:
John Mogford

Telephone:
Croesgoch (03483) 311

SOLVA NECTARIUM

TROPICAL BUTTERFLY FARM AT
SOLVA NECTARIUM LOWER SOLVA

As featured on BBC and HTV television, the 'Nectarium' is an Insect Safari through the grounds of Tan-yr-Allt House, as well as the Insect Galleries in the Old Chapel, Lower Solva.

In our Tropical Glass-House you will walk amidst butterflies from continents around the world, including the rain forests of India, Malaysia and the Amazon. They feed, mate, lay eggs or just lazily fly past you in a hot, steamy, humid 'tropical forest' of continual interest.

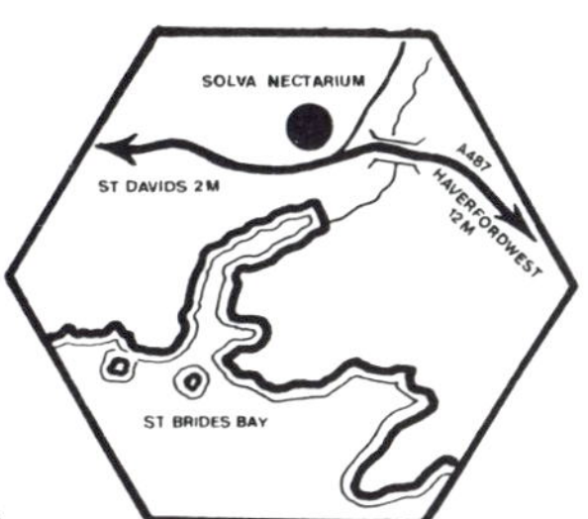

In the Insect Galleries you may watch the live butterflies emerging from their pupae. There are strange caterpillars, live locusts, tarantulas, as well as leaf-cutting ants.

OPEN DAILY: From Easter to end September
Mon - Sat – 10 - 6 p.m.
Sundays 2 - 6 p.m.
Last Admission at 5 p.m.

ENQUIRIES: Telelphone: St. Davids 721323
Detailed information leaflets from all Tourist Information Centres.

South Pembrokeshire

Manor House Wildlife and Leisure Park, St. Florence (090024). One of south Pembrokeshire's most popular attractions. Beautiful wooded grounds, animal and bird enclosures, aquarium, reptile house, playground, shops, model railway etc. No dogs allowed. Tel: 06467-201.
Dylan Thomas Boathouse, Laugharne (090024). Outside Pembrokeshire, but within easy reach. The waterside home of Wales' most famous 20th century poet. Various exhibits about the great man, audiovisual presentation, sales area, tea room. Splendid coastal setting. Tel: 099421-420.
Hoyle's Mouth Cave, near Penally (110003). Not an obvious tourist attraction, but worth a visit nonetheless. Cave used in Palaeolithic times by human hunters who killed reindeer, cave bears, musk-oxen etc. Main chamber is 160 feet in from the entrance. See the *Penally Nature Trail* for notes.
Carew French Mill (043038). The last tidal mill in Wales, with machinery, wheels, sluices in good repair. Due for extensive renovation, but well worth visiting; beautiful site.
West Williamston Quarries (033055). Fascinating relics of the limestone quarrying industry. Several abandoned quarries - also the old "docks" by which barges from the Haven gained access. Not all accessible to the public, but worth exploring.

B. G. and M. BATEMAN

Fresh and Smoked Trout
Fishery Consultants
Wholesale and Retail

VISITORS WELCOME
10 a.m. - 5 p.m.
SEVEN DAYS PER WEEK

FARM SHOP FOR FRESH AND SMOKED TROUT AND PATE

Vicar's Mill, Llandissilio, Clynderwen
Telephone 09912-553

Mid Pembrokeshire

Graham Sutherland Gallery, Picton Castle (010135). Delightful gallery housing the largest public collection of Graham Sutherland works. Castle grounds also open to the public. Tel: 043789-296.
Blackpool Mill, near Canaston Bridge (060145). An impressive 18th century corn mill. Machinery still in good working order, but no milling nowadays. Recently-opened "cave" exhibits in the basements. Tel: 09914-233.
Vicar's Mill Trout Farm, Llandissilio (105224). This trout farm, not far from Clynderwen, is run by Pembrokeshire Fish Farms. Fresh and smoked trout and pâté for sale. Tel: Clynderwen 553.
Tudor Prince Cruises, Hobbs Point, Pembroke Dock (967042). Cruises in a large covered vessel either up the waterway to see the Daugleddau estuary or downstream to see the oil terminals etc. The up-river cruise is magnificent. Tel: Pembroke 685895.

The Ice Age

Many people think that the Ice Age is over and done with. Not a bit of it. We are still in the middle of an ice age which began over 2 million years ago and which is liable to continue for several million years more. The warmish climatic interval in which we live is called and "interglacial" episode, following one period of ice advance and preceding another. This interglacial has so far lasted for about 10,000 years; the climate will get gradually cooler as the next glaciation approaches.

For the greater part of this Ice Age the climate of Pembrokeshire has been cold and snowy, rather like the climate of Iceland or Lapland at the present day. But in the coldest part of each glacial episode the glaciers from the north spread southwards, covering Pembrokeshire and even extending as far south as the Scilly Isles and as far east as the Bristol-Bath area. About 200,000 years ago the whole of Pembrokeshire was deeply buried beneath the ice of the Irish Sea Glacier, Britain's largest glacier. On another occasion, about 20,000 years ago, the ice partly covered Pembrokeshire, extending only as far south as Milford Haven and leaving most of the Castlemartin Peninsula ice-free.

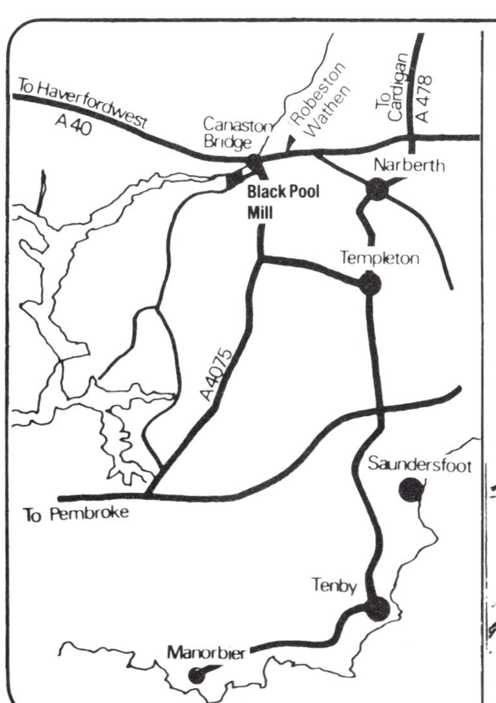

Black Pool Mill and Caverns

Canaston Bridge
Narberth, Dyfed
Telephone: Llawhaden 233

Open:
From Easter to 31st October
(11.00 a.m. to 6.00 p.m.)

PONT HYWEL MILL

SLATECRAFT & PLANTS

Creative slate products - sculptures, sundials, tubs, pots & vases, clocks etc.
House names & nos. engraved.
Commissions & special orders under-taken.
Also alpines, rock-plants, heathers & herbs.
RICHARD & FRAN BOULTBEE, PONT HYWEL MILL, LLANGOLMAN,
CLYNDERWEN, DYFED SA66 7XJ.
PHONE:- HEBRON-09947-543

TOURING IN PEMBROKESHIRE

Top Five Car Tours

The tours which are described on the following pages are fascinating to visitors and contain many stopping-places that may be unfamiliar even to local people. They are described in the barest of detail; for fuller information about towns, villages, and places of interest the reader is asked to consult the Pembrokeshire Gazetteer (pages 69-85), the Islands section (pages 27-31) and the Good Beach Guide (pages 86-91). Also, good maps (preferably Ordnance Survey 1:50,000) are essential. As far as possible, the tours stick to main roads, but here and there detours or sections of tours may require travel on minor or unmarked roads.

Carew Tidal Mill

Tidal Power

Nowadays there is much discussion about the pros and cons of a Severn Tidal Barrage, using the power of the tides to generate electricity. But the use of tidal power is not new. Tidal mills were built in a number of localities in Pembrokeshire, the two best known being at Carew and Pembroke. The Pembroke Mill, which was situated next to the Mill Bridge below the North Gate Tower of Pembroke Castle, was destroyed by fire in 1956, but the Carew Mill still stands in a beautiful site close to Carew Castle. The mill is often referred to as the "French Mill", possibly because the mill stones came from France or because the layout of the mill was based on a French design. There was originally a mill on this site in the Middle Ages, but the present building probably dates from a sixteenth century restoration. From the late 1700's until 1937 the Mill was constantly in use, milling barley and oat meal, wheat flour, bone meal and various fertilizers. At one time there were two working water wheels, each driven by water as it was released through sluice gates from the mill pond. The pond was of course filled at the time of high tide, with the water held back by a substantial stone dam. The mill was saved from dereliction in 1960 and greatly restored in 1972.

The Old Dockyard, Pembroke Dock
Pembrokeshire, West Wales
Telephone: Pembroke 685885

- All rooms have a bathroom or shower, tea and coffee making facilities and some have colour television.
- First class restaurant, noted for its fine cuisine and friendly atmosphere. 2 bars, Sauna and Sunbed all open to non-residents.
- Built in Napoleonic times as the residence of the captain of the dockyard, the Hotel makes an ideal base for exploring the rugged beauty of the Pembrokeshire Coast National Park.
- Ample car parking always available.

Saundersfoot Pottery and Craft Shop

WOGAN TERRACE
SAUNDERSFOOT, DYFED

Visit the Studio and see the Potter Carol Brinton throwing and decorating her pottery, and take the opportunity to browse among hundreds of other craft items for sale in the shop.

Open 10 a.m. to 5 p.m. daily and most evenings throughout the summer season.

Illustrated talks and pottery demonstratiions for parties arranged if you Telephone (0834) 812406.

On the beach at Dale.

Car Tour 1: St. David's and the North-West

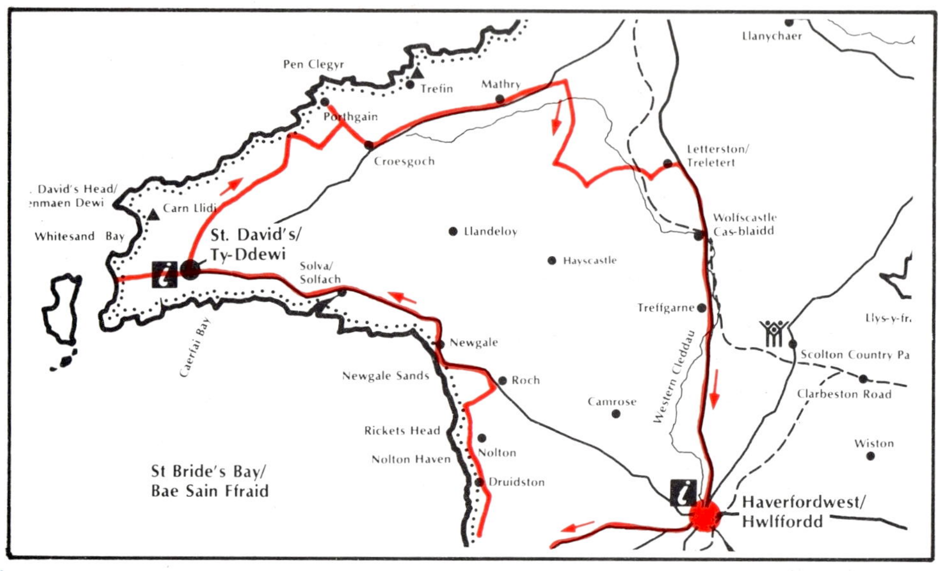

Directions: From Haverfordwest take B4341 to Broad Haven. On sea front turn R towards Nolton on minor road; after Haroldston West take first L to Druidston and Nolton Haven. Drive straight through Nolton towards Newgale; take first R towards Roch. Cross A487 and proceed to Roch Castle *(not open for viewing)*. Return to main road and turn R towards Newgale. *Magnificent views of St. Bride's Bay and Dewisland cliffs.* Through Newgale and continue to Solva, *one of the favourite holiday places of N. Pembs.* As you enter Solva, turn R to Middle Mill, *a pretty hamlet with a woollen mill.* Return to A487. From Solva, continue to St. David's on A487 - *Cathedral, Bishop's Palace, art galleries, cafés, good bookshop, information centre.* Take minor road W to St. Justinian's - *lifeboat station, ruined chapel, lovely views across to Ramsey Island.* Return to St. David's and follow A487 Fishguard road; turn L on B4583 Whitesands road and then bear R along minor N coast road. Turn L to Abereiddi - *Blue Lagoon, old slate quarrying community.* Continue along minor road; at cross roads take L to Llanrian; at cross-roads near church take L to Porthgain - *harbour and fascinating relics of slate and stone quarrying industry.* Return to Llanrian; straight over crossroads to Croesgoch. Turn L on A487. Detour into Mathry - *wood-turner workshop, craft shop, antiques, unusual church.* Continue on A487 for approx. 1 mile; bear R onto minor road, then R at cross-roads, to Llangloffan Farm *(small-scale cheese-making)*. Continue to Castle Morris, take L at cross-roads onto B4331; continue to Letterston. Turn R onto A40, through Wolfscastle and on to Nant-y-Coy Mill - *craft shop, old mill, ample car-parking in lay-by. Easy access to Iron Age Fort and Maiden Castle rocks. Spectacular views over Treffgarne Gorge.* Continue along A40 through gorge; back to Haverfordwest.

O.S. Map Sheet: 157
Distance: approx 98 km (61 miles)
Start and Finish: Haverfordwest

Highlights: Broad Haven Sands and Information Centre; Druidston and Nolton Haven beaches; Roch Castle; Newgale Sands; Solva Harbour, Middle Mill woollen mill; St. David's Cathedral; St. Justinian's and Ramsey Sound; Abereiddi Bay; Porthgain old industries; Mathry village, Tregwynt woollen mill; Llangloffan cheese-making; Letterston village; Nant-y-Coy Mill; Maiden Castle Rocks; Treffgarne Gorge.

Detours: From Broad Haven, drive S to Little Haven village - *beautiful cove with craft shop, inns, good car park, safe bathing.* **From St. David's,** take Porth-clais road to *beautiful little harbour - lime-kilns, magnificent cliff scenery.* **From St. David's,** take B4583 to Whitesands Bay - *golf course, splendid beach, walks to St. David's Head and Carnllidi summit.* **From Mathry,** take minor road NW to Abercastle - *delightful little creek.* **From Letterston,** take 2nd L to S of village towards Sealyham, *home of the Sealyham terriers,* and to Garn Turne - *rocks and burial chamber.* **From Wolfscastle,** take minor road W to Hayscastle Cross, then L along B4330. On top of hill turn R to Plumstone Rock. You are now on the Pembrokeshire Landsker – *glorious views in all directions.*

SEALYHAM ACTIVITY CENTRE

Wolfscastle, Haverfordwest
Pembrokeshire, Dyfed SA62 5NF
Telephone: (0348) 840763

CAMPING or TOURING CARAVANS
SELF-CATERING UNITS

Enjoy an exciting adventure holiday for adults or children or just a peaceful holiday in beautiful Pembrokeshire

ADVENTURE DAYS

Let your children enjoy an exciting day

- Pony Trekking
- Orienteering
- Rockclimbing
- Raft building
- Ropes course
- Canoeing

Sealyham Activity Centre Wolfscastle

Telephone: (0348) 840763

THE COASTAL COTTAGES OF PEMBROKESHIRE

Because we live in and know the area we have been able to choose 100 of the most interesting and spectacular cottages along the quieter areas of the Pembrokeshire coast. Many are on the coastal path with stunning sea views and sunsets, some have a resident heron, badger or fox, even a seal colony. All are close to sandy beaches. Some cottages are luxurious with special awards, others are family-style. All are regularly inspected. Our illustrated brochure gives a fascinating insight into the unchanged world of Pembrokeshire.

Low Season Short Breaks from £45. High Season £165 to £395 per week.
Available all year. Sleeping 2-14 persons. Pets welcomed at most properties.

Abercastle, Pembrokeshire. Telephone 03483 742

Car Tour 2: The Presely Hills

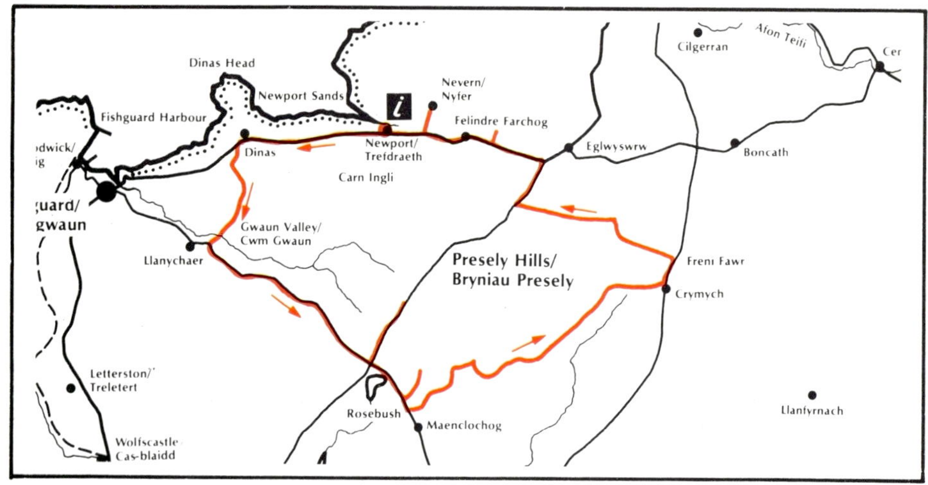

Directions: From Newport take A487 towards Dinas. Just before petrol station turn L and follow minor road onto Mynydd Dinas. *At top of steep hill, small car park/picnic site with wonderful views over N coast.* Continue over the mountain and down to Pontfaen in beautiful Gwaun Valley - *ancient Ice Age meltwater channel.* Across cross-roads, pass Pontfaen Church and bear R to B4313. Turn L and follow B4313 to New Inn - *rolling western Presely Hills, with moorland and forestry plantations.* Turn L at burnt-out pub and drive to summit of Presely ridge, called Bwlch-gwynt. Ample car-parking space. Follow path to west, to summit of Foel Eryr - *National Park/AA direction-finding plaque* (just over ½ mile). Return to car and descend again to New Inn. Turn L at cross-roads onto B4313. Take minor road L into Rosebush - *slate quarries, corrugated iron Precelly Hotel, abandoned railway station, caravan park, ornamental gardens and ponds.* Return to B road; look out for L turn to Crymych, on minor road. Follow minor road to Mynachlogddu. *Magnificent views of southern slopes of Presely; great basin of Cwm-cerwyn, rocky crags, Carn Meini (supposed source of some Stonehenge bluestones), wide expanses of moorland, Waldo Williams Memorial.* Bear L in Mynachlogddu hamlet and continue past Croesfihangel and turn R to Crymych. *Railway settlement; modern secondary school, craft shop, wholefood shop, Bean Machine kitchen.* Take minor road L at lower end of Crymych, towards Pontyglazier and Crosswell. *Views of Foeldrygarn (Iron Age hill fort on summit) and eastern Presely Hills.* In Crosswell, turn R onto B4329. Continue to Penfro Garage; turn L onto A487. Look out for R turn to Castell Henllys - *Iron Age fort and reconstructed round house - a fascinating site.* Return to main road; turn R towards Newport. At Velindre, *see Tudor "College" and cattle pound opposite.* Continue towards Newport. At Temple Bar cross-roads, turn R to Nevern; *a beautiful hamlet; church, Celtic cross, bleeding yew; mounting block; medieval bridge; pilgrim cross; motte and bailey castle.* Return to Temple Bar and continue to Newport.

O.S. Map Sheet: 145
Distance: approx. 70 km (43 miles)
Start and Finish: Newport

Highlights: View of coast from above Dinas; Gwaun Valley; abandoned railway line near New Inn; views of Rosebush Reservoir; Rosebush slate quarries and Victorian "spa" resort; Presely moorlands and crags; Waldo Williams memorial; Crymych - a railway settlement; Castell Henllys Iron Age house; Tudor "College" and cattle pound at Velindre; antiquities at Nevern; Nevern Estuary at Newport.

Detours: From A487 just before Dinas, turn R and take minor road to Cwm-yr-Eglwys - *a very beautiful cove with clean sand and ruined church.* **From Pontfaen,** detour either to E or W for *magnificent valley scenery in Cwm Gwaun.* **From Rosebush,** take B4313 to Maenclochog - *Welsh village with interesting church.* **From Mynachlogddu** take minor road SW to Gors-fawr stone circle. *Not as impressive as Stonehenge, but greatly revered even so!* **From Croesfihangel** follow footpath up onto summit of Foel Drygarn - *magnificent Iron Age Hill Fort with Bronze Age cairns. Splendid views over eastern Presely.* **From Crosswell** take minor road to Newport, passing Felin-y-Gigfran - *very beautiful rocky gorge of Nevern River.* **From Temple Bar** take minor road L and follow signs to Pentre Ifan Cromlech – *magnificent Neolithic Burial Chamber in a most impressive setting.*

The Bluestone Mystery

Everybody knows that some of the inner circle of "bluestones" at Stonehenge are supposed to have come from Pembrokeshire. The three main types of bluestone at Stonehenge are spotted dolerite, rhyolite and volcanic ash, and because (according to some authorities) these occur naturally close together only in one small area around Carn Meini in the Presely Hills, it is assumed that this is where the Stonehenge stones came from. A very elaborate story has been put together to explain the transport of the bluestones on rollers, rafts and dugout canoes over a distance of 180 miles from Presely to Stonehenge. Some archaeologists have become so enthusiastic about the story that they have added all sorts of fanciful elaborations concerning the mathematical and civil engineering skills of people who lived more than 5,000 years ago.

Sad to say (for we all love a nice story) there is not a single scrap of firm evidence to support the theory of the human transport of bluestones all the way from Presely to Stonehenge. It is probably true that some of the bluestones have their origins in the Presely Hills, but we now know that the hills were covered on at least one occasion by the ice of the mighty Irish Sea Glacier, which flowed eastwards up the Bristol Channel as far as the Mendip Hills. The ice carried with it "erratic" boulders and stones from many different areas, and it is most likely that the Stonehenge bluestones were transported for at least part of their journey by glacier ice.

The crags of Carn Meini, reputed to be the source of the Stonehenge "bluestones".

Car Tour 3: Mid-Pembrokeshire

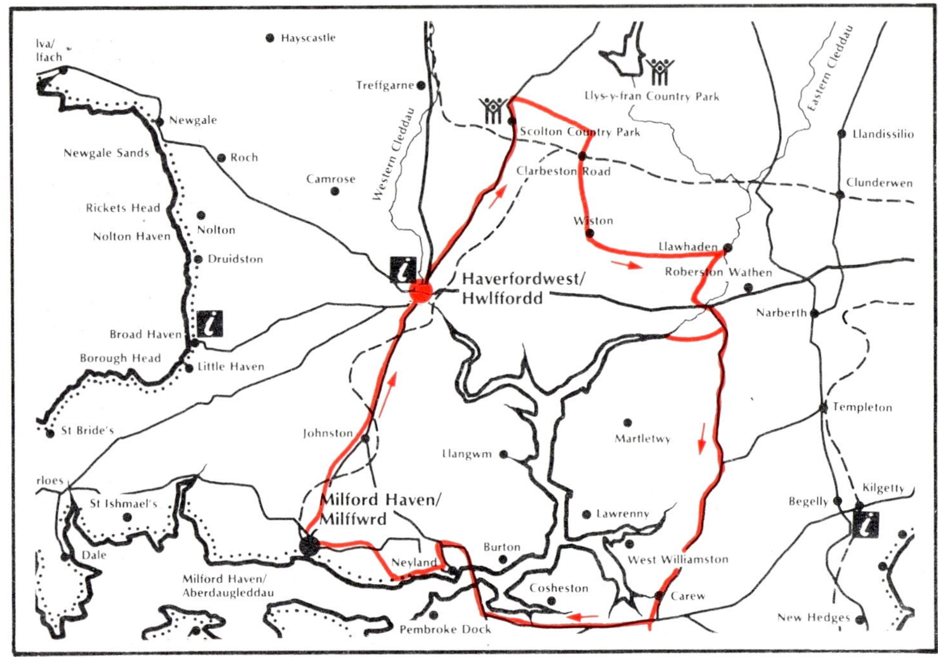

Directions: From Haverfordwest take B4329 to Scolton Manor; just beyond railway bridge, *Country Park, arboretum, museum - well worth a visit.* Continue on B4329, take first R; follow signs to Clarbeston Road and then Wiston. In Wiston, *interesting church and motte and bailey castle with ruined keep.* Take minor road to Llawhaden - *ruined hospitium, magnificent castle, Ridgeway pottery, honey farm.* Take minor road S to Canaston Bridge. Turn L onto A40 then R onto A4075; almost immediately R to Blackpool Mill. *Old corn mill with cave exhibits beneath, milling machinery etc., fine bridge over Eastern Cleddau.* Return to A4075, turn R and continue to Carew - *castle, French mill (last Pembrokeshire tidal mill), and car park/picnic site. Also Carew Celtic Cross.* Continue to A477 cross-roads. Cross over to Carew Cheriton - *fascinating church and ancillary buildings.* Back to A477, turn L and continue to Pembroke Dock. Follow signs to Cleddau Bridge - *box girder bridge over waterway. Splendid views of Haven towns, oil installations. Toll to be paid.* Continue to roundabout, turn L into Neyland. Drive through town and down hill to Brunel Quay - *old passenger port, ferry terminus, rail terminus.* Take shore road W; take first L along minor road past Llanstadwell church to Hazelbeach. *Fine views of the waterway.* Continue to Waterston then Milford. On reaching A4076, either take L into Milford or R towards Johnston and Haverfordwest. En route N, *notice splendid castellated church towers in Steynton and Johnston - typical "Englishry" churches.*

O.S. Map Sheet: 158
Distance: approx. 77 km (48 miles)
Start and Finish: Haverfordwest

Highlights: Scolton Manor Museum and Country Park; Wiston castle mound; Llawhaden Castle; Ridgeway Pottery and Honey Farm; Blackpool Mill; Carew Tidal Mill; Carew Castle; Carew Celtic Cross; Carew Cheriton Church; view of the waterway from the Haven Bridge; Brunel Quay, Neyland; Llanstadwell Church; Gulf Refinery, Waterston; Black Pill; Milford Docks and Hubberston Fort; Steynton Church, Johnston Church.

Detours: From Clarbeston Road follow signs along minor road to Llysyfran Reservoir; *fine walks, fishing, sailing, picnic sites, country park.* **From Canaston Bridge,** take A40 and then B4314 to Narberth - *craft workshops, pottery, bookshop, guest-houses and inns. Old market town.* **From Canaston Bridge,** drive beyond Blackpool Mill to Minwear Wood - *Forestry Commission walk in Slebech Forest.* **Before Carew** turn R off A4075 to West Williamston - *old limestone quarries and oiled birds rescue centre.* **From A477** just before A4075 junction, turn R to Upton Castle - *beautiful grounds open to public.* **From A477** explore Pembroke Dock. **From A4076** explore Milford-Hakin-Hubberston area.

Nantyffin Motel and Restaurant

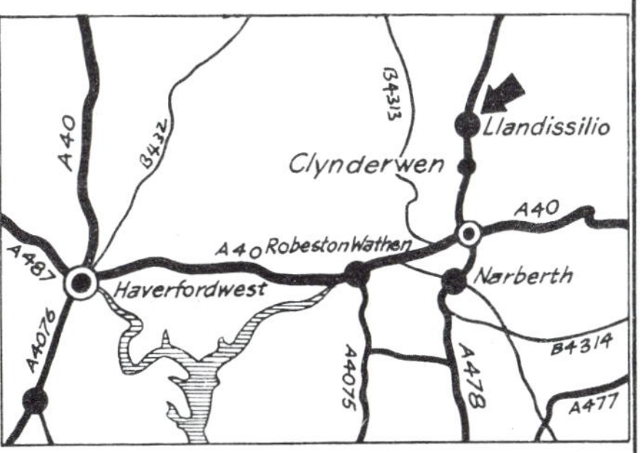

NANTYFFIN MOTEL
& RESTAURANT
LLANDISSILIO - CLYNDERWEN
PEMBROKESHIRE - DYFED
Tel: Clynderwen 329 (Residents 423)

CRAFTS & THINGS

Picton Castle - Haverfordwest

This "one off" Shop never ceases to surprise. Filled with gifts and practical ideas that are colourful, good value for money and always exceptional quality. The emphasis is on the creative ideas of individuals and cottage industries – you are certain to find something quite different and the warmest of welcomes.

Closed every Monday, except Bank Holidays.

VISIT ALSO THE CASTLE GROUNDS AND GRAHAM SUTHERLAND GALLERY.
Please follow the signs to Picton Castle from the A40 road.

something for everyone!

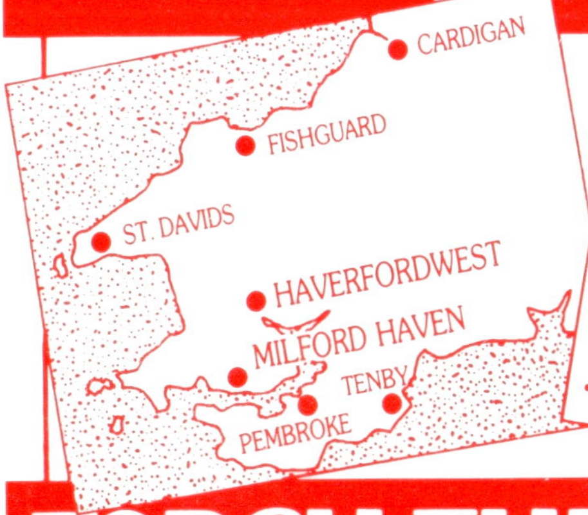

CARDIGAN
FISHGUARD
ST. DAVIDS
HAVERFORDWEST
MILFORD HAVEN
TENBY
PEMBROKE

A strong professional theatre with top acts from the world of jazz, classical and folk music ...hit plays...exhibitions ...films... dance

RING NOW to book and for full season details.

TORCH THEATRE
MILFORD HAVEN 5267

The Drover's Roads

From the 1500's till around 1850 Pembrokeshire figured prominently in the overland trade in livestock. As the demand for meat developed in the growing urban centres such as London, Birmingham and Cardiff, especially after the onset of the Industrial Revolution, there was a ready market for animals "on the hoof" from West Wales. Herds of cattle, sheep, pigs and even geese were driven along a network of drover's roads to Smithfield and other markets. The drovers kept clear of the main highways in order to avoid the payment of tolls on the turnpike roads, to minimise the nuisance to other road users, and to ensure that there was a constant supply of grazing for the travelling animals. Among the collecting centres for animals were Haverfordwest, Eglwyswrw, Boncath, Crymych and Whitland. Many of the resting-places along the way now have inns called "Drover's Arms", as in Puncheston. The routes themselves followed upland valleys wherever possible, and when we see the deeply-rutted tracks across the ridge of Mynydd Presely we can imagine the vast herds of black cattle and other animals that passed this way before the arrival of the railways killed the trade for ever.

Gateposts near Newport

PEMBROKESHIRE CRAFT MARKETS

PCM

is an association of local craftspeople producing handmade items of the highest quality.

Markets are organized throughout the summer at popular resorts

Look out for advertisements or obtain details from Tourist Information Offices or the Secretary: Norman Vessey (Hebron 241)

Pembrokeshire Cottages

Self-Catering as it ought to be

You owe it to yourself to browse through our free colour brochure before you book your Pembrokeshire holiday. ALL our carefully selected cottages and farmhouses provide linen, colour T.V., cots and high chairs free of charge. And we have a higher percentage of Award Winning Properties than any other Agency in the County.

Park House, Tiers Cross
HAVERFORDWEST
Telephone: Broad Haven 764

Deserted Villages

When the Normans and their followers settled in Pembrokeshire they established over 120 new villages and hamlets. Most of these were in "Little England", and many of them grew into quite sizeable places with castles, manor houses, farms and cottages, mills and churches, and other typical features of the Norman manor. The majority of these new villages have survived; examples are Letterston, Cosheston, Hayscastle, Hodgeston, Steynton and Johnston. But in some places changing economic conditions have caused the desertion of old villages so that nowadays few traces can be seen. For example, little now remains of Henry's Moat besides a little church and an overgrown castle mound. Castlebythe, Manorowen, Monington and Picton are now very insignificant settlements, and whatever happened to Walwyn's Castle, St. Twynnells, Flimston, Jordanston, Granston and Bletherston? Why not explore darkest Pembrokeshire for other "abandoned villages"? Telltale signs on the O.S. map are raths or camps, castle mounds, isolated churches and place-names ending in "-ton".

"We went on a mystery tour of the lost villages of Pembrokeshire, but we couldn't find any of them."

Fishermen and lobster pots, St. Brides Haven, 1937

Buy an unusual Present
at the

CENARTH SMOKERY

Smoked Salmon and Sewin
Smoked Beef, Pork and Lamb
Ham, Bacon and Pâté

See sign on Cenarth to Cardigan road — second right after Cenarth

Telephone: LLECHRYD 579

Car Tour 4: The North-East

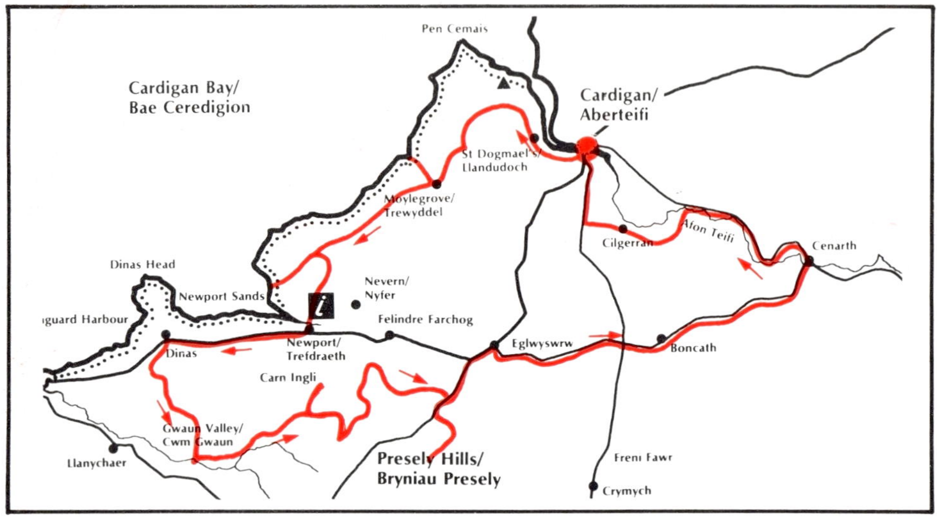

Directions: Cross Cardigan Bridge and turn R onto B4546 to St. Dogmael's. In the village, turn L to see the Abbey ruins and Y Felin - *a beautifully restored working water-mill.* Follow B4546 along Teifi shore to Poppit Sands - *lovely views over the estuary.* At Poppit, *wide sandy beach, fascinating rock formations, café, good car park.* Take minor road to Cippyn and Moylegrove. In Moylegrove, turn R and follow valley to Ceibwr Bay - *a favourite little cove and popular picnic spot.* Continue along minor road towards Newport. Bear R and descend to Traeth Mawr (Newport Sands). *Golf course, sand dunes, car park, the best beach on the N. Pembs. coast.* Return up hill and take R to Newport. *A Norman town-church, castle, large car park, pleasant inns and shops.* Proceed along A487 to Dinas. Turn L before petrol station and drive up steep hill - *old sea cliff dating from time when sea level was +200 ft.* Drive over mountain and descend to Pontfaen. Turn L into Gwaun Valley road. *The most beautiful valley in Pembrokeshire - a relic of the Ice Age.* Sychpant Forestry Commission picnic site and car park on L. Proceed to E end of valley. Drive straight on, following Maenclochog signs up hill. At top, turn sharp L for Crosswell/Brynberian. At cross-roads take L and follow signs to Pentre Ifan burial chamber. *Most magnificent cromlech in Wales.* Continue along minor road; take 2nd R to Crosswell. *Lovely views of Nevern gorge.* Turn L and then take first L (no through road). Drive onto common land - *panorama of N side of Presely Hills and starting-point of Ras Beca cross-country race.* Return to Crosswell and on to Eglwyswrw via A487. In Eglwyswrw take B4332 (turn R) to Boncath and on to Cenarth. *Pleasant rolling N. Pembs. countryside.* At Cenarth, *bridge, falls, fishing, museum, crafts, inn.* Cross bridge on A484 and drive to Llechryd; cross river again on Llechryd Bridge, *near site of old canal and tinplate works.* Follow signs to Cilgerran. *Splendid river gorge, impressive castle, at far end of village entrance to Cardigan Wildlife Park.* Continue to A478; turn R and return to Cardigan.

O.S. Map Sheet: 145
Distance: approx. 104 km (65 miles)
Start and Finish: Cardigan.

Highlights: St. Dogmael's Abbey and Y Felin flour mill; Poppit Sands; Ceibwr Bay; Newport Sands and golf course; Newport Church and Castle (the latter not open to the public); moorland scenery above Dinas, and coastal views of Newport Bay; view of old volcano of Carningli from Cilgwyn; Pentre Ifan cromlech; Nevern valley gorge; Presely Hills scenery from near Crosswell; Cenarth Falls, bridge and fishing museum; Llechryd Bridge; Cilgerran castle, gorge; Cardigan Wildlife Park.

Detours: **From Ceibwr,** walk either N or S along coast path - *magnificent cliff scenery, seals, sea-birds.* **From A487** in Newport, turn R to Parrog - *old sea port settlement, boat club, river estuary, walks along front, large car park.* **From E end of Gwaun Valley,** take L turn into Cilgwyn (signposted "Newport"). Straight on for *Cilgwyn Candles workshop;* turn R for *Woodturner workshop - both "cottage industries".* **From B4332,** E of Boncath, turn R for Cilwendeg - *fine house and parkland (not open to the public).* **From Penrhiw** turn R before bridge for *pleasant drive along sylvan Cwm Cych. Old centre of wood-turning industry.* **From Cenarth,** detour on A484 to Newcastle Emlyn and then on B4333 to Cwm Cou *(Felin Geri mill - working water-driven flour mill).* **From Llechryd,** turn L after crossing bridge for Manordeifi Old Church.

Cardigan Wildlife Park

— FOR A DAY THAT'S DIFFERENT!

It's a fun day out for everyone in unspoilt beautiful Red Dragon country. Whether it's pleasure or leisure, walking or relaxing, you can:

- follow the Nature Trails
- explore the Teifi River Gorge
- study many species of animals
- bird watch from hides
- enjoy river fishing
- relax at the Terrace Café
- picnic in the sun
- buy gifts for your friends
- exhaust yourselves on the Adventure Playground !
- enjoy our evening barbecues
- watch coracle fishing demonstrations

OPEN EVERY DAY. COACHES WELCOME. GROUP RATES

Information: Cardigan Wildlife Park, Cardigan, Dyfed Telephone: (0239) 614449

EATING HOUSE & GALLERY
TEL. DINAS CROSS 508

. . . .

Home Made Fresh Food
Hot and Cold

. . . .

A Selection of Vegetarian Dishes

. . . .

FULL BREAKFAST - MORNING COFFEE
BUFFET LUNCHES - CREAM TEAS
EVENING MEALS – CHILDREN WELCOME

★GALLERY★

Showing Contemporary Paintings and Drawings, including Local Landscape

The Heron Inn

ABERCYCH

A new Inn offering traditional hospitality with two Bars providing Bar Snacks and Restaurant facilities.

Accommodation available all year round.

Ideally situated (2 miles from Cenarth) for exploring the Teifi Valley or Presely Hills

A warm welcome is extended by Stephen and Ann Entwistle

Telephone: Llechryd 229
(Next to the Post Office and Stores.)

Car Tour 5: Tenby and the Castlemartin Peninsula

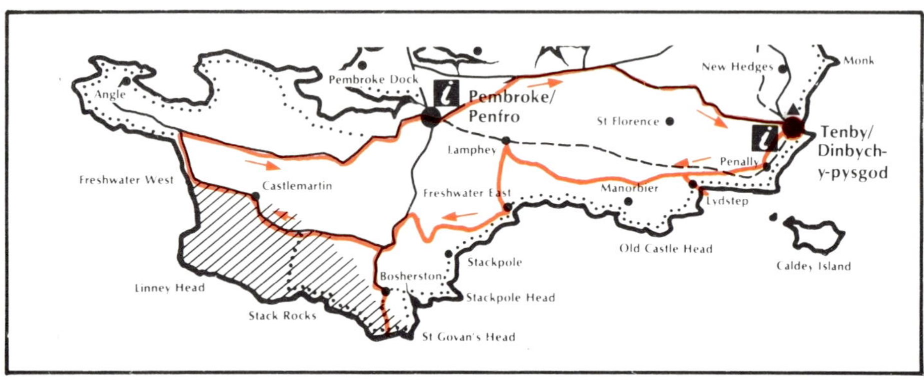

Directions: From Tenby take A4139 towards Penally. In Kiln Park, *magnificent multiple lime kiln designed by John Nash.* Proceed to Penally, just off main road. *Interesting church, pottery, inns etc.* Continue to Lydstep - walk down the headland, *see Smugglers Cave, walk around Nature Trail. Splendid cliff scenery, with views of Caldey.* Continue on A4139 to Lamphey - turn R to Bishop's Palace. *Fortified Bishop's residence with parkland.* Return through village and take B4584 to Freshwater East. Turn R along minor road down to beach car park. *Splendid sands but untidy developments.* Continue on minor road to Stackpole *(National Trust projects in progress)* and continue to B4319. Turn L and then L again to Bosherston - *interesting church, café, inn.* Walk to Lily Ponds; *if time, follow path to beautiful Broad Haven beach.* If road is open, continue along minor road to St. Govan's Chapel. *Old monastic cell in a cleft in the limestone cliffs. Magnificent cliff scenery.* Return to B4319; take L, continue past Merrion camp; take 1st L to Stack Rocks and Green Bridge of Wales. *Classic site for limestone cliff scenery.* Also Flimston *deserted settlement, now inside MOD range.* Return to B4319. Continue to Castlemartin *(cattle pound roundabout!)* and to Freshwater West. *Superb beach; seaweed drying hut; sand dunes.* Continue to T junction with B4320. Turn R, continue to Hundleton, passing entrance to Orielton Field Centre *(interesting residential courses).* Continue into Pembroke - *castle, churches, town walls, mill pond, good shops, gypsy caravan museum, crafts.* Take A4075 from east end of town; continue to Sageston, turn R on B4318. At Minerton, *Manor House Wildlife and Leisure Park* - a fascinating and popular place for a break. Continue towards Tenby - *note modern windmill to R of road.* At Gumfreston, *pretty Norman-style church.* Back into Tenby.

O.S. Map Sheet: 158
Distance: approx. 76 km (47 miles)
Start and Finish: Tenby

Highlights: Kiln Park limekilns; Lydstep headland and Smuggler's Cave; Lamphey Bishop's Palace; Bosherston Lily Ponds; St. Govan's Chapel; Green Bridge of Wales and Stack Rocks (scenery and nesting sea-birds); Castlemartin cattle pound; Freshwater West beach and seaweed-drying hut; Monkton Priory church; Pembroke Castle, town walls, gypsy caravan museum; Manor House Wildlife and Leisure Park; Gumfreston church.

Detours: From Tenby, opposite Kiln Park entrance, turn R along minor road for Hoyle's Mouth cave. **From Lydstep,** turn off A4139 onto B4585 to Manorbier; *magnificent castle, interesting church, fine sandy beach.* **From Bosherston,** take minor road to Broad Haven Sands - *beautiful unspoilt beach, white limestone cliffs, large car park on clifftop.* **From B4319,** minor roads R to St. Twynnels, Warren and Castlemartin churches - *all interesting examples of "Englishry" church architecture.* **From Freshwater West,** take B4320 to Angle village, shore of Angle Bay, and West Angle Bay - *each place fascinating.* **From B4318,** just before Manor House Park, turn R to St. Florence - *delightful S. Pembs. village with Flemish chimney etc.*

Lamphey Palace

OUR "TRADITIONAL" RANGE
OF
FARMHOUSE DAIRY ICECREAM
CONTAINS
ONLY THE FINEST
NATURAL INGREDIENTS.

AVAILABLE IN A VARIETY OF
UNUSUAL FLAVOURS
FROM OUTLETS THROUGHOUT
PEMBROKESHIRE.

"KISMET"
and
D.S. ENGRAVING
(NEW!)

Willings Passage
Pembroke 685718

Browse at your leisure at "Kismet" – the "in" place for all jewellery, clocks, watches, leather goods and the unusual.

D.S. Engraving – offering sports trophies and engraved gifts for men.

ENGRAVING ON THE PREMISES
"POP" ITEMS ALSO IN STOCK

PEMBROKE CASTLE

This outstanding Norman Castle, standing on a rocky promontory at the western end of Pembroke's main street, is bounded on three sides by a tidal inlet of the Milford Haven Waterway. The Castle, a massive limestone fortress, was begun in the year 1105, and was the birthplace of Henry VII. Its outstanding feature is the Keep, which is 75 feet high with walls 16 feet thick.

OPENING HOURS

Easter to end of September: Open every day including Sunday 9.30 a.m. to 6.00 p.m. (gates close 5.30 p.m.).

WINTER PERIOD

October to Easter: Monday to Saturday 9.30 a.m. to 4.00 p.m. (gates close 3.30 p.m.). Closed Sundays, Xmas Eve, Xmas Day & New Year's Day.

ADMISSION CHARGES – Adults 80p – Children and O.A.P's. 40p.

These charges will not apply on limited occasions when special events are taking place in the castle.

THE ABOVE TIMES AND CHARGES ARE CORRECT AT TIME OF GOING TO PRINT

A carefree day out for the whole family
at

Manor House Wildlife and Leisure Park

St. Florence, Tenby Tel: Carew (06467) 201
(on the B4318 Tenby - Pembroke road)

"WALES IN BLOOM" WINNERS 1983, 1984 and 1985
A HOST OF OUTDOOR AND INDOOR ATTRACTIONS
SET IN 12 ACRES OF DELIGHTFUL WOODED GROUNDS

Birds and animal gardens
Aquarium and reptile house
Tropical plant house
Children's playground
Picnic and snack area
Model railway exhibition
Gift shop
Falconry displays daily (exc. Sat.)
Pets corner
Cafeteria and licensed bar
Mini Marina - radio controlled boats
Giant slides and roundabouts - Rides
Go-Kart track - Radio controlled Go-Karts

Party bookings, senior citizens and children and reduced rates
Open daily (including Sundays) 10 a.m. - 6 p.m.
Easter until September   Ample free parking for cars & coaches
IT IS REGRETTED THAT NO DOGS ARE ALLOWED

Top Five Walking Trails

If you do not feel energetic enough to tackle the whole of the Pembrokeshire Coast Path (about 180 miles long), there are a number of stretches where circular cliff walks can be undertaken. Good examples are the walk around North Hill, Angle, starting and finishing in Angle Village; and the walk around the Deer Park to the west of Marloes. Many other splendid walks are described in the NPA *Trails* **leaflet, the Preseli** *Walking* **leaflet, and the South Pembrokeshire** *Rambles around Tenby* **leaflet. These list the main self-guiding trails for which publications are available, varying from walks of one mile or less to the 7-mile walks around the Dale Peninsula and Llysyfran Reservoir. For disabled visitors the NPA has published an excellent booklet (***The Disabled Visitor's Guide***) which details, with the aid of very clear maps, 19 short routes which are full of interest and free of wheelchair obstacles.**

The five trails which are briefly described below are personal favourites of the author. If you try them, they may whet your appetite for the scores of well-marked routes to be followed in the coastal and inland districts of Pembrokeshire. Please note that O.S. 1:50,000 maps are essential if you are to follow the described routes without difficulty and if you are to obtain maximum enjoyment from your walks.

1. Dinas Island (approx. $3^1/_2$ miles)

One of the most popular walks on the north Pembs. coast. Visitors should note that Dinas Island is not an island at all - it is simply a promontory which is almost cut off from the mainland by a deep Ice Age meltwater channel.

Start and finish: *either at Pwllgwaelod (at the western end of the valley) or at Cwm-yr-Eglwys (at the eastern end). Car parks at both places.*

Main features: *The footpath is well marked and reasonably safe - some slippery sections on the eastern side of the headland. Note the treeless aspect of the western (exposed) side of the headland and the relatively lush vegetation on the eastern (sheltered) side. Birds and plant life are described in a WWNT leaflet, available from information centres. Nesting birds include fulmars, shags, ravens, gulls, razorbills and guillemots, and other birds to be seen include gannets, choughs, oystercatchers and cormorants. The highest point on the footpath, at Pen-y-fan, is 463 ft above sea-level, and is located at the northern tip of the peninsula. From here, magnificent views towards Fishguard, across Newport Bay, and southwards towards the mainland cliffs with the hillmass of Carningli beyond. This walk is at its most beautiful in May and June when bluebells, sea campion and thrift are in bloom.*

Stackpole Quay

2. The Golden Road (Presely Hills) (approx. 7 miles)

Far and away the most impressive inland walk in Pembrokeshire. The ancient track follows the main ridge of the Presely Hills; the B4329 Haverfordwest-Cardigan road conveniently crosses the ridge between the summits of Foeleryr and Foelcwmcerwyn, and cars can be left adjacent to the road on a firm, grassy parking place. The walk is not a difficult one, but walkers should be prepared for cold wet weather and for soggy conditions underfoot in places.

Start and finish: *either at Bwlch-gwynt (on the B4329 road) or at Croesfihangel on the minor road W of Crymych. Ample parking space at both ends. Transport will have to be arranged to take you back to your starting point.*

Main features *(described W-E): Large-scale forestry plantations on S side of ridge; Ice Age landscape of moorland and frost-shattered rocks and glacial erratics to N. Detour S off track to summit of Foelcwmcerwyn. Bronze Age burial mounds. To E of summit, an old slate quarry in the face of Craig-y-cwm (the site of Pembrokeshire's last glacier remnant, about 10,000 years ago). Return to main track near Foelfeddau and follow "the Golden Road" E, past the fantastic rocks of Cerrigmarchogion, across the col (note the rutted tracks of the old Drover's road) and up to Carnbica. Just beyond the tor, Bedd Arthur, one of the many graves of King Arthur (in reality the remains of a Neolithic burial chamber?). To the N, on the flank of the ridge, the splendid tors of Carngoedog, Carnbreseb and Carnalw. Proceed across the next col to Carnmeini, the famous source of the Stonehenge spotted dolerite if you believe our archaeological brethren. Stonehenge apart, this is a marvellous tor. Follow the well-beaten track E and then take the track through the heather to the summit of Foeldrygarn - Bronze Age tumuli and a splendid Iron Age fort with embankments, ditches and hut circles. Descend directly to Croesfihangel, weary but exhilarated.*

Foel Drygarn Hill Fort.

The Trewern Arms

Nevern, near Newport

The Friendly Inn by the River

Restaurant specialising in Fish Dishes open Tuesday to Saturday Evenings
Grill Room open daily for Bar Meals and Snacks
Family Lunches on Sundays – 12.30 - 2.00 p.m.
Bed and Breakfast

FOR ENQUIRIES AND RESERVATIONS PLEASE TELEPHONE:
NEWPORT 820395

The House of Good Food and Hospitality

3. Slebech Forest Walk (approx. 1 1/2 miles)

This walk is totally different in character from the Dinas Island and Presely walks; it follows a woodland trail within a mixed woodland now managed by the Forestry Commission. The path is gently undulating, never far from the road, and in general well sheltered by the trees; this means that the walk is a convenient "bad weather" walk. It can also be combined with visits to Blackpool Mill, Picton Castle or Llawhaden on a day trip from any of the main holiday centres. A Forestry Commission leaflet about this walk is available from information centres.

Start and finish: *car park to the right of the minor road less than half a mile beyond Blackpool Mill.*

Main features: *Viewpoint from car park across Eastern Cleddau valley and towards Blackpool Mill and Llawhaden Castle. Start walk across the road. Japanese larch plantation, Douglas fir plantations, Norway spruce, rhododendrons, broom; also woodlands composed of oak, birch, alder, willow, hazel etc. Wildlife traces of badgers, foxes, hedgehogs, squirrels, and possibly otters. Flocks of starlings at some times of the year. Along the edge of the river, swans, mallard, cormorants, herons, kingfishers etc.*

Right:
Eastern Cleddau coracle fisherman

AT LAST! - THE POWER TO CUT FUEL BILLS-
PERMANENTLY.

LOW COST
SOLAR HEATING
SYSTEMS
FULL SYSTEMS FROM ONLY £600

DAYSTAR

- ★ Is inexpensive to install
- ★ Is efficient
- ★ Uses natural free energy
- ★ Adds value to your property
- ★ Is manufactured locally to highest British Standards
- ★ Provides a quick return on your investment.

For further information (without obligation) contact Cambrian Developments, Unit 1A, Gelligeirios Industrial Estate, Cwmffrwd, Carmarthen. Tel: (0267) 230999

4. Bosherston Circular Walk (approx. 3 1/2 miles)

A very attractive walk which brings in St. Govan's Chapel, St. Govan's Head, Broad Haven and the Bosherston Lily Ponds. You will see something of the coastal platform of the Castlemartin Peninsula, but the cliff scenery of this area is the real focus of interest, impressive and savage when a good stiff south-westerly wind is driving waves against the cliffs. The idyllic watery environments of the Lily Ponds, en route back to Bosherston, are totally different in character.

Start and finish: *Bosherston village. Car-parking may be a problem in the summer; if Bosherston is full to overflowing leave your car at the Broad Haven car park instead and use this as your start/finish point.*

Main features: *From Bosherston take the road signposted to St. Govan's Chapel. (Before setting out, check that the road is open; it crosses the MOD firing range and may be closed at certain times of the year). Notice how flat the landscape is - this is an old wave-cut platform cut at a time of higher sea-level. Take a close look at St. Govan's Chapel - a fifth century hermit's cell recently restored and tidied up by the NPA. If you like, detour W for a few hundred yards on the coast path to look at the Huntsman's Leap and other incredible wave-cut gashes in the limestone cliffs. More spectacular scenery on St. Govan's Head (messed about by the Army) and around New Quay. Nesting sea-birds on the cliffs near here. Broad Haven is a lovely bay - see page 86. Descend to the sands and follow the path from the N corner of the bay into the magical world of the Lily Ponds. Cross the 3 bridges and return up the lane to Bosherston church and hamlet. If you need refreshment, the inn and café will look after you.*

Stalactites in a Pembrokeshire limestone cave

Below: Bosherston Lily Pools in high summer

Carnedd Meibion Owen, near Newport

5. Gwaun Valley Walks (approx. 9 miles)

It is now possible to walk on carefully maintained footpaths all the way from Lower Town Fishguard to Croesfihangel, near Crymych. The eastern part of this walk is described as "The Golden Raod" walk on page 84, and is well known to the walking fraternity. The western section, opened in 1984, is less well known but is equally dramatic in landscape terms. It is centered on the magnificent Gwaun Valley, a deep channel cut by sub-glacial meltwater some 200,000 years ago and renowned among landscape scientists and geologists as the classic British example of its type. The valley is very beautiful, with wooded sides up to 200 feet high and a wide range of vegetation types. Parts of the ancient woodland are protected as Sites of Special Scientific Interest, and others are managed by the NPA and the Forestry Commission. Much of the valley floor is farmed, and there are small communities centered on the hamlets of Llanychaer and Pontfaen.

Start and finish: *either at Lower Town Fishguard (adjacent to the road bridge) or at Bwlcj-gwynt on the B4329 road. Ample car-parking at both ends, but return transport will have to be arranged. Shorter (circular) walks can be started from Pontfaen, Dan Coed or Tregynon. Total distance: approximately 9 miles.*

Main features *(described west-east): follow the footpath signposted on the floor of Cwm Gwaun from Lower Town to Llanychaer. Nearby, old slate quarry at Cronllwyn and a magnificent example of a Flemish Chimney at Garn. Follow the footpath signs to Cilrhedyn Forestry Commission car-park and picnic area. Marked walk in Forestry Commission woodland. Continue, passing once derelict Llanychlwydog Church to Pontfaen —.a small hamlet with a pretty church across the river, a famous pub (the Dyffryn Arms), and a Baptist Chapel and graveyard. Eastwards from here, two routes to choose from —.one at the foot of the woodland and one along its upper edge. Fine views of the valley from the upper route. Circular route from Dan Coed around a steep side valley with waterfalls and dense deciduous woodlands. The main Gwaun Valley route climbs through Coed Tregynon past Tregynon Camp (probably an Iron Age earthwork) to Tregynon Farmhouse (teas available). Follow the drive to Ty-gwyn; cross the road and take the path to Penlan-wynt, uphill to Foel Eryr (NPA viewing pointer) and down to Bwlch-gwynt car-parking area. Fine views in all directions from Foel Eryr.*

GAZETTEER TO TOWNS, VILLAGES AND OTHER PLACES OF INTEREST

Please note: Every effort has been made to ensure the accuracy of the following entries. However, if you spot any errors, the publisher would be delighted to hear from you and corrections will be incorporated in the next edition of the guide. Mention of places and buildings in the text does not guarantee that they have free public access; intending visitors are asked not to wander onto private land unless there are clear public footpath signs etc.

Abercastle (853336). One of north Pembrokeshire's little ports, bustling with coastal trading activity prior to the coming of the railway age. Cargoes included grain (note the ruined grain-store above the creek), limestone, coal and luxury goods. Now there are only pleasure boats and small fishing boats on the beach. Easy access by car. Nearby is the famous Carreg Samson cromlech (848335), well worth a visit.

Abereiddi (796310). An attractive bay on the northern coast of the St. David's Peninsula. Old slate-quarrying industry; note the Blue Lagoon (a flooded quarry pit) and the ruined quarrymen's cottages, quarry buildings and quay. A mineral line used to run along the valley to Porthgain. Pretty cottages close to the sea - this is a favourite spot among artists. Easy car-parking adjacent to the beach.

Amroth (163079). A seaside village which suffers much from coastal erosion. It marks the point at which the Landsker reaches Pembrokeshire's south coast. The castle is an eighteenth-century replacement for the original. The church, some way inland, was enlarged and rebuilt around 1856. Colby Lodge, built at the end of the 1700's, was designed by John Nash and is located in a wooded valley rich with rhododendrons and hydrangeas.

BROAD HAVEN HOTEL

BROAD HAVEN
Nr. HAVERFORDWEST
DYFED (Pembrokeshire) SA62 3JN

Telephone: Broad Haven (043783) 366

Opposite beautiful beach. All 35 bedrooms with private bathroom/shower, colour T.V. (with video films), radio/intercom/baby listening, tea trays. Heated Swimming Pool with sunbathing terraces around. Solarium. Bars. Mother's Room. Games Room. Outside Table Tennis. Pool Table. Soundproofed Dance Hall.
Dinner, Bed and Breakfast weekly £104 - £139. Please write or phone for full colour brochure and holiday pack.

Angle (865030). A single-street village at the western end of Angle Bay. On the main street the Georgian-style Globe Hotel catches the eye, but there are far more interesting buildings here, including the church, a little fisherman's chapel built in 1447, a pele-tower castle. a dovecote with a domed roof, and Angle Hall a little way to the east of the village proper. The tidal creek to the east of the village is muddy and is no place for bathing, but it has a certain charm about it, and visitors can see the last remains of five old sailing vessels slowly rotting away on the beach. Across Angle Bay can be seen the Texaco refinery and the BP Ocean Terminal, with more massive oil storage tanks close to sea-level at Kilpaison. The BP offices are housed in Popton Point Fort, built in 1863. There are other forts in the vicinity at Chapel Bay and on Thorn Island. Close to the beach in West Angle Bay there is an old brickworks.

Bosherston (966948). A neat little village near the south coast of the Castlemartin Peninsula. The parish churchyard has a 14th century Cross bearing the head of Christ at the intersection. Nearby features of interest include the popular Bosherston Lily Ponds, St. Govan's Chapel, and the delightful Broad Haven (South) beach.

Broad Haven (860135). One of the finest beaches in Pembrokeshire. "The Haven", as it has always been known to Haverfordwest people, became a fashionable resort early in the last century. The cliffs both to north and south of the main beach are of great interest to geologists, showing spectacular structures in the Coal Measures. There has been much recent housing development. The resort is well blessed with hostels, guest houses and caravan sites, and the new Youth Hostel and Pembrokeshire Countryside Unit are added attractions.

Carew (048037). One of the most delightful places in Wales - picturesque and interesting, and with a timeless appeal for the visitor. There are two main centres of interest. Around the head of the tidal creek we see the Carew Celtic Cross (a fine example of an Early Christian decorated monument), Carew Castle (started in the 13th century and extended and improved in the 15th and 16th centuries) and the Carew tidal mill. On the other side of the river is an attractive and spacious picnic site and car park. Half a mile away, on the other side of the A477, Carew Cheriton Church is well worth a visit. There is an old chapel in the churchyard, and the Old Rectory is a building with many ancient features.

Teifi Corcale fisherman

D. G. THOMAS & Son Ltd.

Builders Merchants
Cilgerran
Cardigan
Telephone: 614141/2

A small family business in which service counts. Try us for all your building requirements. Same-day or next-day delivery service.

Also all grades of coal supplied.

Castlemartin (915983). An earthwork and cluster of houses not far from the great bay of Freshwater West. The roundabout in the middle of the village is the old cattle pound - take a look at it if you can without disrupting the traffic! The church, down a lane to the north, has a battlemented tower, and the organ once belonged to Mendelssohn. On the eastern side of the churchyard is a ruined building called "The Old Rectory" about which hardly anything is known.

Cenarth (269416). Strictly, just outside Pembrokeshire, but a favourite place with salmon fishermen and holidaymakers. Here the waters of the Teifi rush over a cataract into deep rock pools, and even when the river is not in flood it is both beautiful and impressive. There used to be coracle netting here - but the ancient craft has now been killed off by the protests of the angling fraternity. The old stone bridge is a fine example of the bridge-builder's art, just like that at Llechryd further downstream. Also at Cenarth - a small Victorian church, an old mill, a craft shop and a fascinating fishing museum.

Cilgerran (194430). An elongated village above the gorge of the River Teifi. The castle is justly famous, having been portrayed (among others) by the artists Richard Wilson and J.M.W. Turner. The massive fortress, built of slate slabs and with impressive drum towers, was built in 1093. It is well maintained and is well worth a visit. Cilgerran is the venue for an annual Coracle Regatta. Just outside the village is the entrance to the Cardigan Wildlife Park, now under new management following the splitting up of the Coedmore Estate.

Cosheston (004037). An elongated village of a classic Norman type, with ancient strip fields running perpendicular to the main street. The church is interesting, with a slender tower and octagonal steeple. Nearby Upton Castle has attractive grounds which are open to the public.

Crymych (184339). There was not much in Crymych before the arrival of the railway in the year 1875. Then the settlement expanded rapidly to become a thriving agricultural service centre. The A478 passes through, but the railway is no more. The chief architectural feature is the monumentally ugly *Ysgol Preseli*, a comprehensive school serving a wide area of the Welshry.

Cwm-yr-Eglwys (015400). A picture postcard settlement with pretty cottages, lush vegetation and (occasionally!) a beach of golden sand. One of the most beautiful bays in Pembrokeshire, in the lee of Dinas Island and opening eastwards into Newport Bay. This is the old "Dinas Harbour" used by coastal trading vessels and fishing boats since the Middle Ages. At one time there was a flourishing trade in slates from the sea quarries on the cliffs to the east, and there was also a ship-building industry. The old church close to the shore was destroyed in October 1859, during a great storm that sank over 114 ships around the coasts of Wales. The ruins of the church have recently been made safe, and the massive new sea wall should ensure that the sea encroaches no further along the cwm. Car-parking is very limited at Cwm-yr-Eglwys, and access is via a steep and narrow minor road.

Anne & John Jones

BWYD-Y-BYD

Telephone: Crymych 537

- Wholefoods
- Spices
- Dairy produce
- Variety of cheeses
- Fresh fruit and veg
- Herbal remedies
- Books

FISHGUARD MARKET THURSDAYS

DISCOUNTS ON LARGE QUANTITIES

Cwm-yr-Eglwys: the ruins of the old church

SERJEANTS INN

Eglwyswrw

Free House
Accommodation
Restaurant

Restaurant open
7.30 - 11.30 p.m.
3-course Sunday Lunch

BOOKINGS CROSSWELL 271

Dale (810058). One of the most popular sailing centres in Pembrokeshire, located inside the entrance of the Milford Haven waterway and enjoying a sheltered position in the lee of the Dale Peninsula. Once a thriving ship-building and trading centre. Nowadays the Dale Yacht Club organizes sailing races throughout the summer, with a regatta during August. Dale Sailing Company provides a chandlery service and much else besides. Note that the beach is stony rather than sandy, and that there is a lack of car-parking space. Dale Castle is modern rather than ancient, and is not open to the public. Much more interesting is Dale Fort, one of the Victorian defences of Milford Haven, well preserved and used as a field study centre. The road from the western end of the village takes the motorist past the old Kete airfield and to St. Ann's Head lighthouse and coastguard station.

Dinas (012389). A straggling village on the A478 east of Fishguard. The village runs along the foot of the steep northern slope of the Carningli-Mynydd Dinas upland. Millions of years ago the coastal strip hereabouts was beneath the sea, and breakers crashed against the cliffs some 200 feet above present sea-level. You can still see the old stacks and cliff-face crevices from the road, together with spectacular meltwater channels cut during the Ice Age. The parish church, built in 1860, is at Brynhenllan. To the north is Dinas Island, so called because it is almost an island, separated from the mainland by a deep glacial meltwater channel. The walk around this headland is magnificent, and it is described on page 64. Dinas Island is the locale for two of R.M. Lockley's books, namely *Island Farmer* and *Golden Year*.

Eglwyswrw (142385). The village, named after "the church of St. Wrw", lies approximately mid-way between Newport and Cardigan. The church is in a circular, pre-Christian churchyard. Interesting buildings include the Sergeant's Inn with the tiny courtroom next door, and a moated manor house called The Court which was the house of David Martin, Bishop of St. David's around the year 1300.

Fishguard (958370). North Pembrokeshire's main shopping centre, occupying an undulating clifftop site and linked to the villages of Abergwaun (Lower Town) in the mouth of the Gwaun Valley and Goodwick around the terminus of the railway line. Lower town, which must surely be one of the most attractive coastal settlements in Wales, was once a busy shipbuilding and herring-fishing centre, and it is still popular with fishing and boating enthusiasts. The main town owes most of its growth to the last 150 years. There is a good shopping centre, and the Market Square is the centre of affairs. The Royal Oak Inn claims the distinction of having been the place where the surrender papers were signed following the Last Invasion of Britain in 1797.

Freshwater East (885990). A large bay located about 2 miles south of Lamphey. There is a fine sandy beach backed by sand dunes, but the settlement is a shambles, spoiled many years ago by haphazard chalet developments. There is now a comprehensive development plan in force, and the County Council wishes to concentrate various types of holiday accommoadtion here. Reasonable access to the beach, but a shortage of summer parking.

Freshwater East

For Your
Holiday Hair Appointment

Telephone: 873393

The Hair Studio
4 West Street, Fishguard

Freshwater West (885994). A magnificent bay in the far west of the Castlemartin Peninsula. Glorious empty sands, massive sand dunes, and fascinating rocky shores to explore. Frainslake Sands, in the south, lies within the Army firing range and is out of bounds. Do not bathe here - there are high waves, currents and undertows. There are also quicksands in places. Close to the road you can see a restored seaweed collector's hut - once used for drying the special seaweed destined to become laver bread.

Goodwick (945382). A large village at the head of Fishguard Bay, with streets and houses clinging to the steep eastern slopes of Pen Caer. Once a sleepy fishing village, the settlement expanded rapidly around the turn of the century with the development of the rail terminal and the harbour designed for trans-Atlantic liner traffic. The high hopes of the developers were unfulfilled, but the port became (and remains) an important one for Irish ferry traffic. Sealink vessels transport containers and other traffic, and passengers , between Fishguard and Rosslare daily. Goodwick has a pleasant sandy beach and its sheltered waters make it a popular boating centre. The Last Invasion of Britain occurred hereabouts in 1797, and the defeated French soldiers laid down their arms on Goodwick Sands. High on the headland above the harbour is Harbour Village, built around 1906 by the GWR as a railway workers settlement. The most imposing building in Goodwick is the Fishguard Bay Hotel, now thriving after a chequered history. Behind the Frenchman Motel is the site of the old Goodwick Brickworks, which closed in 1969.

Seaweed Drying Hut

Until quite recently a number of Pembrokeshire beaches were used for the gathering of the seaweed which is transformed into "laver bread". Freshwater West was one such locality and close to the road on the headland at the southern end of the beach stands the last of the seaweed collector's huts. This little hut, like the 20 or so that stood in the vicinity half a century ago, was used to dry the seaweed before it was washed and then boiled to produce the slimy delicacy so beloved by all civilized people. Within the last few years the hut has been rebuilt and rethatched using the original thatching technique.

Welsh Place Names

In north Pembrokeshire (the Welsh-speaking area) it is natural that the majority of place-names should be in Welsh. However, even in the southern area which has been anglicised for 900 years, many of the English place-names have Welsh equivalents, and according to County Council and Welsh Office policy sign-posts now generally display Welsh and English names together. The following brief list may help you to interpret some of the commonest Welsh place-name elements:–

aber	mouth of
afon	river
allt	wood, slope
bach (fach)	small
bedd	grave
cae	field
caer	fort
capel	chapel
carn	cairn
carreg	stone
castell	castle
coch	red
coetan	quoit
craig	rock
cwm	valley
dinas	hill-fortress
dyffryn	valley
eglwys	church
foel	bare hill
glas	blue
glyn	deep valley
gwaelod	bottom
gwaun	upland valley
gwyn	white
hafod	summer place
isaf	lower
llan	holy place
maen	stone
maes	field
mawr (fawr)	great, big
melin (felin)	mill
morfa	bog, sea-marsh
mynydd	mountain
newydd	new
ogof	cave
pen	head, top
pont	bridge
porth	harbour
rhos	moor
traeth	beach
tref	homestead
ty	house
uchaf	higher
ynys	island

Hook (978115). Once the centre of a coal-mining district. Hook colliery was the last anthracite mine in Pembrokeshire to close, in 1948. Now there are few traces of the mines or railway tracks which once dominated the area, although two old quays can still be seen. There are a few ancient cottages, but most of the development is modern.

Haverfordwest (955155). This is the old county town, located at the lowest bridging-point on the Western Cleddau and just below the tidal limit of the river. The castle on the hill was one of the two major fortresses of the Norman colony, built originally before 1120. The Normans built a walled garrison town with town gates, splendid churches (dedicated to St. Thomas, St. Mary and St. Martin), and busy trading quays. Most traces of the town walls have disappeared, but the town is full of features of interest. St. Mary's Church is one of the finest churches in Wales. The Castle, destroyed by Oliver Cromwell and later housing the County Gaol, is now the interesting Castle Museum. There are two bridges over the river; the basin between them was once used for the unloading of cargoes of culm and limestone, but is now a large sterile car park. Along the river the old quays and warehouses (and the "Bristol Trader" inn) remind us of the town's great trading traditions; in Tudor and Stuart times this was one of the most important ports in Wales, but the coming of the railway in 1853 killed off the trade in general goods. Two of the town's most interesting ruins are down-stream of the town - the Augustinian Priory and Haroldston House. The town itself is full of interesting buildings - the Shire Hall, the Masonic Hall, Foley House (designed by John Nash), and the nonconformist chapels are well worth looking at. Of the modern buildings, the new Riverside Market Hall is probably the best - a commercial white elephant, maybe, but attractively designed and located. The main shopping streets nowadays are High Street and Bridge Street; Quay Street, along the river, was once the slum quarter but is now greatly uplifted.

Johnston (933105). A large and not very attractive village located where the A4076 road crosses the main railway line south of Haverfordwest. The church is a classic "Little England" building with a tall tower. Johnston Hall was once the home of the Kensington family.

Kilgetty (125073). A sprawling and somewhat untidy place which was once a coal-mining village but which has grown rapidly in recent years as a result of the Tenby-Saundersfoot holiday boom. Chiefly botable nowadays for a large supermarket, a well-appointed Information Centre (run jointly by the National Park Authority and the South Wales Tourism Council), AA and RAC breakdown centres, and a glassmaking workshop.

Lamphey (016005). A very old village, chiefly notable for the splendid Bishop's Palace once used as a residence by the Bishops of St. David's. The remains of the palace are well looked after by Cadw (Welsh Historic Monuments), and are set in carefully landscaped parkland. Nearby, the imposing Lamphey Court is now a hotel. The church in the village has a Norman tower, but was largely rebuilt in the nineteenth century.

Haverfordwest Quay in the early 1900's

COME
AND WATCH
THE ART OF
GLASSMAKING AND
GLASSBLOWING
AVONDALE GLASS
Glass fruit, vases, dishes, paperweights, animals and many souvenirs of Wales – all made entirely by hand.
Visitors welcome. *Admission Free*
Glassmaking: Mon, Tues, Thurs, Fri
8.00 a.m. to 2.30 p.m.
Wed. 8.00 a.m. to 1.00 p.m.
Avondale Glass, Kilgetty, Nr. Saundersfoot
Tel: Saundersfoot 813343

Keeston Kitchen
Licensed Restaurant
Music every night.
Phil on guitar,
Clare on pots and pans!
Open at lunchtimes.
Phil and Clare Hallet offer a mouthwatering choice of home cooked food and excellent wine in friendly surroundings. We have a take-away service offering some of our more popular dishes ... all at realistic prices.
On the A487 Haverfordwest/St. Davids Road.
Telephone: Camrose 710440

DYLAN THOMAS' BOAT HOUSE

Telephone:
Laugharne
(099420) 421

Winner of Prince of Wales Award

Sitting Room with original furniture and photographs, audio and video presentation, Tea Room, Art Gallery and small Shop.

The one time water-side home of Wales' most famous 20th century poet.

Located 4 miles south of A40 on A4066 near St. Clears.

OPEN: 10 a.m. to 6 p.m. every day from Easter to November.
Adults 60p; Children and OAPs 40p.

HAVE A DAY OUT TOGETHER BY TRAIN ON THE LOCAL SOUTH PEMBROKESHIRE LINE

There are lots of interesting places to visit with a cheap day return ticket.

For full details please enquire at Pembroke Dock, Tenby, Haverfordwest or Whitland Stations or call in at your local British Rail Appointed Travel Agent

Landshipping (020112). A quiet backwater near the confluence of the two Cleddau rivers. Once a great anthracite mining district, the community was shattered by the Garden Pit Disaster of 1844. There were two quays here. Landshipping Quay proper was the local exporting point, while the little quay on the shore of the Eastern Cleddau was used by the ferry from the Picton side.

Laugharne (300105). Strictly, this little town lies outside Pembrokeshire, but it is a favourite place with south Pembrokeshire holidaymakers. It was originally a Norman town, and its stone fortress was used to defend the eastern routeway into Little England. The site is magnificent, with the castle and streets clustered in a little embayment on the western side of the Taf estuary. The estuary is now so silted up that only small pleasure craft can use it. Besides the castle, the church with its battlemented tower is a reminder of the town's Norman links. Also, a number of ancient traditions survive in the organization of town life. Laugharne is remembered above all else nowadays as the place where Dylan Thomas, the wayward poetic genius, lived and wrote some of his best work. His Boathouse, along the cliff walk behind the castle, is now open as a little museum, run by the South Wales Tourism Council.

Lawrenny (017069). An attractive old village well off the beaten track, with some pleasant cottages and a church with a tall tower. The road along the Cresswell River shore has windblown oak trees, and out on the point Lawenny Quay (once an important coal exporting point) is now a popular yacht station and marina. Some of the holiday developments are not particularly attractive.

Laugharne, on the Taf Estuary

Letterston (940297). A long village (with its axis running across the A40) to the north of Haverfordwest. Once a Norman manor ruled by one Letard, by all accounts a very unpleasant Fleming. The village is very similar in form to Cosheston in the south. At one time an important cattle market, Letterston owes most of its growth to the railway era, with the junction of Pembrokeshire's two Fishguard lines just to the north of the village.

Little Haven (856128). A charming village nestled into a cove at the south end of Broad Haven beach. Once a coal-mining centre, the village is now given over to tourism. It has a safe sandy beach and is popular with sailors and other sea sport enthusiasts. The church is at Walton West, up the steep hill to the east.

Llanfyrnach (220312). A hamlet to the SE of Crymych. Surprisingly, in such a Welsh area, the church has a tower. There used to be much industry hereabouts - traces can be seen in the abandoned lead workings NE of the hamlet and in the massive slate quarry at Glogue.

Llangwm (990093). This village with a Welsh-sounding name is located deep in the heart of the Englishry. For centuries the name has been pronounced "Lang-gum" and the locals will take great offence if you try to Welshify it. The original settlers here were either Norse seafarers or Flemings - whoever they were, the place developed a reputation for clannishness and resentment against outsiders. Now all that has changed, and the village has much modern development and many immigrants. Located on the west bank of the Daugleddau estuary, Llangwm was inevitably a fishing village, with local people making a living from herrings, oysters and cockles. During the 1800's and early 1900's there was much trade connected with the coal industry, and many local men worked at the Pembroke Dockyard. There is a village green, with a Victorianised bellcote church nearby. From Blacktar Point there are glorious views of the estuary, and cockles can still be dug from the mud.

Llanstadwell (006050). Sometimes referred to as Hazelbeach, this is a real sea-front village, strung out along the shore road between Neyland and Waterston. There are pretty cottages and a fine church with a tower right at the water's edge. The beach is stony and muddy, but this is a popular place among boating enthusiasts. Across the water is the old Pembroke Dockyard, and the B & I passenger vessels pass close to the shore every day.

Llanwnda (933395). A fascinating hamlet with a boulder-strewn rough "village green" (with remnants of stone circles on it?) and a simple unpretentious bellcote church. There has been a church here since early Christian times, and Asser, the friend of King Alfred, was educated here. There are a number of inscribed stones in the vicinity, and prehistoric remains are abundant.

AUCTIONEERS, ESTATE AGENTS AND VALUERS

J.J. MORRIS

PROPERTY SHOWROOMS AND OFFICES AT

FISHGUARD
16 MAIN STREET
Tel: 873836 and 872653

CARDIGAN
BROYAN HOUSE, PRIORY ST.
Tel: 612343

Our professional experience within the Pembrokeshire area extends over half a century, involving Residential, Holiday, Commercial, Industrial and Agricultural Property.

It will be our pleasure to be of service to you.

THE CRAFTMANSHIP
Little Haven

- Woodwork
- Pottery
- Soft toys
- Jewellery
- Leather work

– all made by craftsmen here in Wales.

Open Easter - September (Mid July - September open evenings)

CREAMPOTS FARM
TOURING CARAVAN AND CAMPING PARK

Broad Haven, Haverfordwest

Telephone: 043783 - 359

Level site. Easy access from B4341 (Broad Haven) road or from B4327 (Dale) road.

H & C water, showers, flush toilets, shaver and hairdrier point, fully equipped laundry room, children's play area. Milk and eggs available daily.

WITHIN EASY REACH OF THE GOLDEN BROAD HAVEN SANDS

Llawhaden (070174). This is an old frontier settlement, located close to the Landsker. The castle was a fortified Bishop's residence, strongly sited and further protected by a moat. Most of the ruins date from the thirteenth century. Down by the river, there is an interesting church dating from the 1380's, and there is a ruined hospitum at the far end of the village. The Old Mill is now a trout farm, and the village also has an interesting pottery.

Llysyfran (040244). Nowadays the whole place is dominated by the reservoir, built originally to ensure a good water supply for the Milford Haven oil industry. The little church has strong associations with Howel Davies, one of the best-known Pembrokehire evangelists of the 19th century religious revivals.

Lydstep (087983). Unusual, in that the village was largely built by the first Viscount St. David's, who also built a large house for himself in Lydstep Haven. Nowadays the land along the shore is a large and beautifully landscaped caravan site. In the village are the ruins of the mysterious medieval Palace of Arms. The headland is National Trust property; car park and nature trail. Lydstep Caverns can be explored at low tide.

Olive Leaf
Bookshop

133 Charles Street, Milford Haven
Telephone: 4103

A wide variety of Christian Books, Cards and Crafts including Bibles and Children's Books

MILFORD HAVEN CHRISTIAN FELLOWSHIP SERVICES

Sundays 10.30 a.m.
in the Hall adjoining the Shop

For other meetings enquire at Shop or telephone

Maenclochog (083274). A large village in the Presely foothills - very Welsh, in spite of the Norman appearance of the church tower. The centre of the village is taken up with a spacious village green and a raised churchyard. The settlement has a rather grotesque collection of building styles, but it is a fascinating place.

Manorbier (066978). Gerald the Welshman's birthplace and favourite place still has the feel of the Middle Ages about it. The castle is delightful, looking more like a crusader fortress than an Anglo-Norman stronghold. The bay, with its beach, sand dunes and red cliffs, is on an intimate scale, and parts of the church are even older than the castle. Well worth a visit.

Marloes (785075). For many years a quiet and self-contained village; nowadays alive with visitors during the summer months en route for Marloes Sands and Skomer Island. There are some pretty cottages in the village, but the main features of interest are the strange clock tower and the little church. Marloes Sands are magnificent, although no vehicle can approach the beach. Musselwick Sands, also somewhat difficult of access, are becoming popular nowadays. Martin's Haven, which has only a stony beach, is the departure point for the Skomer Island boats.

Mathry (880320). The village is perched on a hill summit, enjoying wide views over the north coast and Pen Caer. The church (on a prehistoric circular site) is very unusual - massive and squat. A good centre for holidaymakers, with a wood-turners workshop, an antique shop, and farmhouse teas.

Milford (905060). In 1790 Sir William Hamilton, a local landowner, obtained permission from Parliament to establish a market and port close to the old settlements of Hubberston and Pill. So Milford was born, built largely through the initiative of Sir William's agent Charles Greville. In the early days the commercial growth of the port was connected with the sperm-oil industry, run by a group of Quaker whalers from Nantucket. There was also a Naval Shipyard here, but this moved to Pembroke Dock in 1814 and Milford never developed as a successful port in its own right. The docks were not completed till 1888, but during the early part of this century Milford was one of Britain's main fishing ports. After years of stagnation the town received a great boost with the coming of the oil industry in the late 1950's and 1960's. Now oil refineries dominate the skyline and jetties dominate the waterway. The town itself is pleasant and airy - carefully planned (as befits a "new town") with three parallel main streets and with large housing areas across the pill in the Hubberston-Hakin area. St. Katherine's Church (1808) is devoid of charm, but far more interesting is the little fisherman's chapel accessible from The Rath - this may be one of the oldest religious buildings in Pembrokeshire. In Hakin there is a ruined Observatory, but the most interesting local building is Hubberston Fort (one of "Palmerston's Follies") next to the Conservancy Board H.Q.

Monkton (980014). Now a suburb of Pembroke, Monkton was once an important part of the Norman settlement. The lofty, spacious church was once a priory church. Monkton Old Hall is a fifteenth-century building. Most of the old priory buildings have disappeared, but there are some traces in Priory Farm, including a dovecot.

Llysyfran Reservoir

South Pembrokeshire Dialect

Following the colonisation of south Pembrokeshire by the Normans and their followers in the eleventh century, English replaced Welsh as the language of everyday use. It has remained the language of "Little England Beyond Wales" ever since. But the spoken English was by no means Standard English; over the centuries it endured as a dialect unlike any other, incorporating Welsh and Anglo-Saxon words, French words, Flemish words, and dialect words from Ireland, Devon and Cornwall and further afield. These are some of the words that the visitor might still encounter in common use today:–

Drang: a passage or narrow alley

Couple: a few or several

Tamping: exceedingly angry

Lake: a stream

Pill: a tidal creek

Tupp: silly, foolish

Caffled: entangled

To pile: to throw

Kift: clumsy, awkward

Rab: broken shale

Tump: a small mound

Popple: a pebble

Skew-whiff: on the slant, crooked

To traipse: to plod, to wander aimlessly

Trash: hedge cuttings

To scaddle: to scatter small objects about

Now just: a little while ago

DID YOU KNOW ..

that the River Cleddau once had its own particular type of coracle, made with a squared-off bow and flat bottom?

that 200 years ago furze mills were quite common in Pembrokeshire, producing chopped gorse for animal feed?

that Pembroke Dock was once the largest flying-boat base in the world, used by the Sunderland aircraft of RAF Coastal Command?

that in the 1920's and 1930's rabbit catching was an important rural activity, with many train-loads of rabbits leaving from Pembrokeshire railway stations every week?

that Henry Tudor, later to become King Henry VII, was born in Pembroke Castle?

R.K. LUCAS & SON

ESTABLISHED IN PEMBROKESHIRE SINCE 1789

Auctioneers, Estate Agents, Surveyors and Valuers

The Tithe Exchange
9 Victoria Place, Haverfordwest
Tel: (0437) 2538 and 5404
and
36 Charles Street, Milford Haven
Tel: (06462) 5713

Clerks to the Sir John Perrot Trust.

Restaurant and Country House for Guests
EAST STREET - NEWPORT - PEMBS.
Newport (0239) 820575

Come and eat with us in our Restaurant, run by the family – Eluned, John, Judi and Mike. We think you will like us – you may know us – so do try us !

Morning Coffee - Teas with a Welsh flavour. Interesting wholefood Lunches our Speciality (Egon Ronay Recommended)

Dinner at Cnapan will offer you an imaginative and varied menu which we promise will be good. Bookings advisable.

Bed and Breakfast for those who would like to stay. Please ring for current Rates.

Moylgrove (117447). Set deep in the valley which runs out to the coast at Ceibwr, the village is full of character. The architecture is a mixture of ancient and modern. So many of the cottages are holiday homes that the village almost dies in the winter. Ceibwr is a pretty bay, but there is no sandy beach and very little parking.

Mynachlogddu (145305). A little hamlet in the heart of the Presely Hills, surrounded by bleak moorlands, forestry plantations and stony barren hills. Above the hamlet are the rocky crags of Carn Meini (the supposed source of some Stonehenge bluestones), and a little way to the west is the simple memorial to Waldo Williams, one of Pembrokeshire's best known Welsh poets.

Narberth (110147). Originally a defended castle town, this is now a thriving service centre for a large area of eastern Pembrokeshire. The castle, dating from 1246, is in ruins and is not open to the public. There are some fine buildings in the town, including the Town Hall and Magistrate's Court. The church tower dates from the 1200's, but the rest was rebuilt in 1879. There are a number of interesting craft workshops in the town today.

Nevern (083401). One of the prettiest hamlets in Pembrokeshire. There is an interesting motte and bailey castle on the river spur above the hamlet, but the focus of interest lies in the beautiful grouping of church, vicarage, old school, bridge, inn (the "Trewern Arms") and cottages around the river; and fields, paddocks and wooded slopes are essential parts of the settlement. The church, with its squat Norman tower, is full of interest. In the churchyard the massive St. Brynach's Cross (dating from the 10th century AD) is much photographed, while visitors also flock to see the famous bleeding yew trees which shade the path to the church door. Outside the churchyard gate there is a mounting-block for horsemen, and halfway up the hill to the west there is an ancient pilgrims cross engraved in the solid rock.

Newgale (850220). Nowadays a favourite holiday resort, with caravanners, campers and day trippers flocking in to enjoy the two miles of firm, golden sand. The massive storm-beach, made of pebbles from far and wide, is more interesting than the beach, and at times of severe winter weather remnants of the ancient "submerged forest" may be stripped clear of their covering of sand. The valley running inland has marked the position of the Landsker for many centuries.

Newport (057392). Once the chief centre of the barony of Cemais, this is a Norman town in the heart of the Welshry. Note the Norman castle (much modified and now used as a private residence), the church (with a solid Norman tower), and the old mills which used to depend upon water power. The town was given a charter before 1215, and ancient traditions are still lovingly preserved; the Court Leet meets regularly, and the Mayor (appointed by the Lady Marcher) has to perform various duties during the year. One of these is to ensure that the parish boundaries are in order, and the annual Beating of the Bounds ceremony takes place during August. The Newport area is well blessed with prehistoric monuments, and the cromlech called Carreg Coetan is located in the town, incongruously fenced off at the edge of a small housing estate. Parrog is a part of Newport nowadays, but during the last century it was a self-possessed seafaring community, with its sailors and merchants, its shipbuilders and its fisher folk. Some of the old warehouses remain, and the Boat Club stands as a maritime symbol out on the old slate-built quay. Now the estuary is silted up, and pleasure craft occupy all the moorings. The holiday industry is now of great importance to Newport, and the town is able to capitalise on its wonderful scenic resources - river estuary, Traeth Mawr (the finest sandy beach on the N. Pembs. coast), sand dunes, magnificent sea cliffs, wooded valleys, and the rocky eminence of Carningli as a backdrop.

Neyland (965051). Brunel's 1856 choice for the terminus of the South Wales Railway, Neyland was supposedly destined for greatness as a port. It did act as the terminus of the Irish steam packet service until 1906 and there was also a local fishing industry, but it never attracted the transatlantic steamers. During the first half of this century Neyland was very much a railway town, with its wagon-works providing much local employment. In 1955 the rail depot closed, causing a great deal of local distress. There was a ferry service until the opening of the Cleddau Bridge, but now most of the road traffic across the haven by-passes the town. Part of Pembrokeshire Technical College is located here.

Nolton (860186). The village is a little way inland. It has a bellcote church and not much else of interest. Nolton Haven is a popular holiday beach, but visitors are probably unaware that this was once a coal-exporting beach. Note the remains of the old coal quay, built in 1769. Traces of the long-abandoned coal mines can be found all over the area; some of the coal workings ran far out under the sea.

SOMEWHERE SPECIAL

for your next holiday

Trefelin Fach is a charming stone-built self-catering Cottage (sleeps 2-4) on a smallholding in the National Park, about 2 miles from Newport and the sea. Adjacent to the Gwaun Valley and the Presely Hills.

- ★ Available all year
- ★ Electricity included
- ★ Linen provided
- ★ Solar heating
- ★ Wood burning stove
- ★ Radio; Colour T.V.
- ★ Local book collection
- ★ Craft courses by arrangement
- ★ Fresh spring water
- ★ Free range eggs
- ★ Goats milk
- ★ Garden produce

Contact: Mrs. Inger John
Telephone: Newport (0239) 820470

Old buildings at Parrog, Newport (Richard Withers).

CROESO I TREFDRAETH!

The people of Newport extend the warmest of welcomes to visitors. The town (called Trefdraeth in Welsh) is an Ancient Borough with its own Mayor, Burgesses and Court Leet. It is a perfect holiday centre. Not far from the old coastal trading quays there is a glorious sandy beach and holiday activities include sailing, golf, and pony trekking. Prehistoric sites, a Norman castle, craft workshops, and abundant wildlife are added attractions.

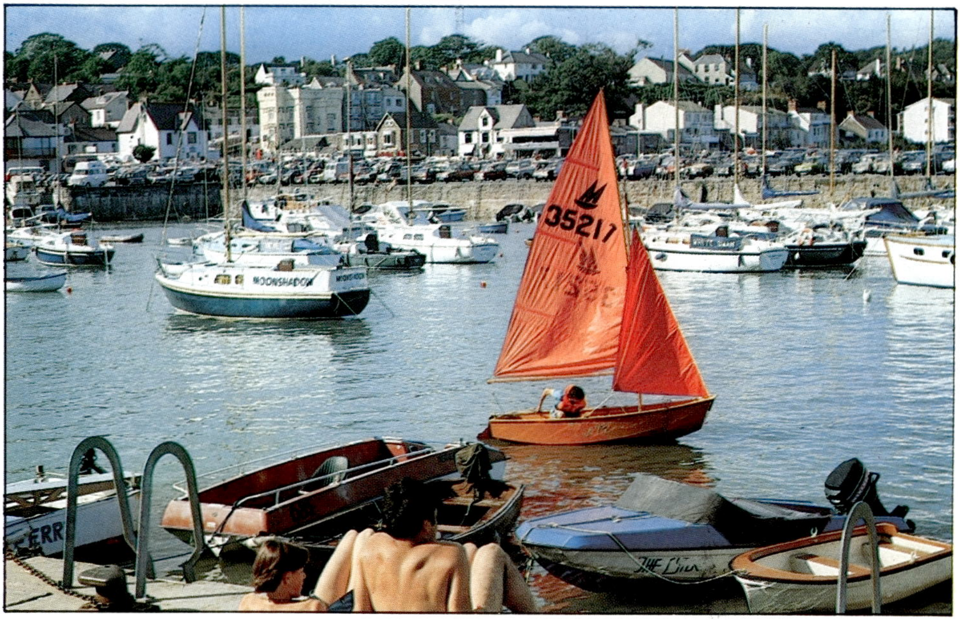

Saundersfoot Harbour at high water

ROSEMOOR
Country Cottages

**Rosemoor Nature Reserve
Pembrokeshire Coast
National Park**

Our comfortable Cottages, with full gas central heating, are furnished and equipped to provide care-free holidays. Each has a conventional oven, micro-wave, pressure cooker and crock pot, and you have a choice of delicious home-cooked meals from our freezer as well. You can stroll through the Nature Reserve or opt for fly-fishing on our well-stocked lake. Open all year with especially low winter rates.

You deserve a Rosemoor Holiday: Why not come and inspect us?

**Rosemoor, Walwyn's Castle
HAVERFORDWEST
Telephone: Broad Haven 326**

IT'S THE NEAREST THING IN FISHGUARD TO THE ODEON, LEICESTER SQUARE!

THE
STUDIO
CINEMA
FISHGUARD

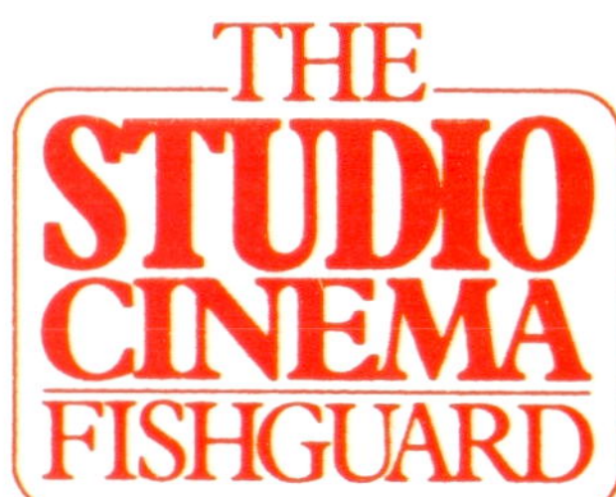

West St. Tel: 873421

TREAT THE FAMILY TO A FILM!

Pembroke (919179). In the early days of the Norman colony this was the chief town of Little England. Its main feature was the massive castle, begun about 1190 and completed over a period of a century or more. The castle, which never fell to the Welsh, is still remarkably well preserved, although its present appearance owes much to restoration work over the past century or so. The most impressive feature of the castle is the Great Keep, among the finest circular keeps in Britain. Close to the main entrance is the Henry VII Tower, believed to have been the birthplace of Henry Tudor in 1456. Beneath part of the castle there is a large natural cavern called The Wogan. The castle was linked by strong walls to the fortified town, which was strung out along a limestone ridge. Many remnants of the town walls can still be seen, and the town still has a medieval feel to it. The Pembroke River is impounded by a dam beneath the North Gate Tower, and there used to be a tidal mill on the quay. There are a number of interesting old buildings in the town, including the 13th century St. Mary's Church (greatly restored), the massive Methodist Cahpel, and the ancient buildings around Monkton Hill. Close to the large car parks on the south side of the town there is an interesting Gypsy Wagon Museum.

Pembroke Dock (966034). The town grew up with the Royal Naval Dockyard from 1814 onwards. Laid out on a gridiron plan, most of the town's housing is undistinguished, and the most striking features of the urban landscape are connected with the dockyard and its defence. The dockyard still dominates the waterfront even though most of its large buildings have gone. There are splendid Martello Towers at either end of the dockyard, and above the town the massive Defensible Barracks looks as solid as it ever did in the days of Queen Victoria. The dockyard closed in 1926, and since that time the town has suffered severe depression, relieved partly by a military presence during the Second World War. The was a Sunderland flying-boat base here, and this was the starting point for hundreds of Atlantic convoys. The town paid dearly for its military involvement, however, for the oil fuel storage tanks (still dominant features of the town) were attacked on many occasions by enemy aircraft, culminating in the Great Tanks Fire of 1940. There are a number of small factories in the town, and at the western end of the town the massive stack of the CEGB Pembroke Power Station is hard to miss.

Pendine (235082). Just outside Pembrokeshire, but a popular place because of its four-mile stretch of sand. The beach is backed by dunes and marshes, and some way inland is an ancient abandoned cliffline, followed by the road to Laugharne. The village is a mottly collection of buildings, with the oldest part on top of the hill. The army has taken over most of the local area, preventing direct access to the eastern end of the beach. The sands were used on many occasions by the great speed-record drivers of the past.

Penally (118991). Village on a spur overlooking Tenby golf-course and the sea. The church is of interest, particularly for the elaborately-decorated Celtic Cross now located in the south transept. Behind the Penally Arms Hotel are the ruins of the medieval St. Deiniol's Chapel. St. Teilo, one of St. David's contemporaries, is thought to have been born here, and there was once an important monastery somewhere in the vicinity.

TUDOR PRINCESS FOR HAVEN CRUISES

Sailing from Hobbs Point, Pembroke Dock. 5 Times a Day – Plus Evenings

* Special Party Bookings for 30 - 120 Persons with full buffet if required *

Licensed Bars on two decks – rain or shine we cater for all ages, including disabled.

Our Cruises offer either scenic beauty of the National Park up river, or spectacular Refinery installations down river, which are especially attractive at night.

10% Discount to individuals presenting this advertisement at the Booking Office for regular cruises.

Picton (010135). The castle is magnificent, set in parkland and occupied by the Philipps family. It was built around 1300, and a four-storey block (in the best possible taste) was added in 1800. The castle now houses the Graham Sutherland Gallery, and this and the gardens are open to the public. Down the road Picton Ferry, on the shore of the Eastern Cleddau, is an idyllic picnic spot.

Pontfaen (022341). A picturesque little settlement in the Gawun Valley. The church, on the valley side south of the river, is on a miniature scale and has four 9th century memorial stones in the churchyard. The Dyffryn Arms is *the* Gwaun Valley public house, famous for its home brew. The newly opened Gwaun Valley Trail to Tregynon starts in Pontfaen.

Porthgain (815325). A place full of character, crammed with relics of the local Industrial Revolution. Porthgain Village Industries was largely responsible for the development of the old slate quarry and for the workings of the igneous stone quarry out on the open coast. In the first two decades of this century Porthgain was a hive of activity, with the little harbour heavily used and with steam coastal vessels exporting slate, bricks, and various grades of crushed stone to many of the ports of southern England. By 1931 all operations had ceased. But we can still see the quays, the stone hoppers, the remains of the stone-crushing plant, the ruined engine shed, the traces of clifftop railway tracks, and much else besides. Note also the lime-kiln and the beautiful little row of quarrymen's cottages. Now in the care of the NPA, the future of this important little hamlet is in good hands.

Rhoscrowther (905023). A little hamlet now totally dominated by the Texaco and BP Oil installations. The church, in a cluster of cottages, old rectory and council houses, is of Norman origin, with a corbelled tower. There is a little annexe to the church which was possibly once the cell of St. Decuman. On the edge of the Texaco refinery is Eastington Farm, an ancient building with a square tower and parapet, probably of Norman age. This was Eastington Manor, one of Little England's minor fortresses.

Roch (881212). Once an attractive Anglo-Norman settlement centred around the the 13th century peel tower castle, perched high on a crag of rhyolite. The castle was the birthplace of Lucy Walter, mistress to Charles II and mother of the ill-fated Duke of Monmouth. The nearby church, in its circular churchyard, and the fine farm buildings opposite the castle, are also attractive, and there is a trace of a village green. But the western end of the settlement is a disaster, with bungaloid ribbon development all the way to the A487.

Rosebush (074293). The spa that never was. Rosebush hardly existed in 1850, but with the arrival of the Narberth Road and Maenclochog Railway in 1876 there was a great spate of development. The slate quarries on the slopes of Presely were extended, a quarryman's row of cottages was built to house workers and the landowner, Sir High Owen, determined to set up a local tourist industry. Lakes were excavated, and fountains, streams and ornamental gardens were designed for the delight of holidaymakers. But the waters proved to be very ordinary, and the place never became a spa. The quarries closed soon after

Pembroke Unicorn Carvery

THE COMMON, PEMBROKE
Telephone: (0646) 685759 or 686224

Traditional Sunday Lunch
Full English Menu
and Traditional Chinese Menu
Children's Menu available
Take Away Service
Seating up to 170

Licensed Restuarant
Large Car Park Opposite

Coach Parties Welcome

Open daily including Bank Holidays from 10.30 a.m. to 9.30 p.m. (Last Orders)

1900, the railway declined in importance, and the holidaymakers declined to come. Rosebush is now a place full of relics and memories, with the deserted quarroes, the abandoned railway station, and many other features of interest to the industrial archaeologist. The corrugated iron Precelly Hotel is well worth a visit, and the owner of the caravan park is working hard to resurrect some of the former glory of Rosebush as *the* touring centre of the Presely Hills.

Rosemarket (953084). A large South Pembrokeshire village, overlooked by most of the guide-books. Once an important market, the village has an Iron Age hill-fort, a Celtic-style Church, and (unusually) a network of village streets.

St. Bride's (803109). A little cove on the southern shore of St. Bride's Bay, with a church (greatly restored by the enthusiastic Victorians), a limekiln and a couple of houses. Once an important trading point for this rocky stretch of coastline. Between the church and the sea is an early Christian cemetery, and traces of stone-lined graves are visible in the cliffs. Kensington Mansion, to the west, was built around 1800 by Lord Kensington. For many years it was used as a hospital.

St. David's (753252). This, the smallest city in Britain, is a place devoted to the memory of Wales' patron saint. The first monatery was built here in the sixth century, but the present cathedral dates from Norman times, having been commenced in 1182. The building in its present form is a concoction of styles and the result of rebuilding and restoration work over 800 years or so - the most recent major projects having been in 1789 and 1863. But the cathedral is undoubtedly magnificent, almost hidden from view in its little valley, encircled by its massive wall and cheek-by-jowl with the ruined Bishop's Palace and the 13th century St. Mary's College. The latter building, in ruins for centuries, was restored and opened again for public use in 1966. In spite of some distinctly unpleasant developments on the main street, St. David's is still an attractive breezy place, with shops, inns, and houses grouped around a spacious square which leads via The Pobbles to the Cathedral's Tower Gate. The area around the little city is full of interest, with prehistoric sites, sites connected with the religious history of the peninsula, the scenery of striking beauty around the coast. Little wonder that St. David's is still a place of pilgrimage today.

St. Dogmael's (165460). A fishing village on the Teifi estuary, much enlarged over the last 150 years by housing developments. The site is beautiful, with houses clinging to steep hillsides above the water. St. Dogmael's Abbey was founded in the 12th century; the ruins are now well looked after, and are full of interest. The spacious parish church (dating mostly from 1847) occupies part of the old abbey site. Opposite the entrance to the Abbey is Y Felin, a restored flourmill, which is now in full production. The mill wheel is driven by water from the millpond and the old machinery can be seen in operation.

St. Florence (083012). A pretty village with houses and cottages grouped around the church. The whole place has a real "Little England" feel about it. Note the old Flemish chimney on the roadside. Gardens are a blaze of colour during the summer, and the village has an enviable reputation as a winner in the annual "Wales in Bloom" competition. Not far away is the Manor House Wildlife and Leisure Park.

St. Ishmael's (835073). A village on the north shore of Milford Haven, not far from Dale. There is an old motte north of the village, but the main feature of interest is the little church, located away from the village in an idyllic valley ornamented with windblown trees and shrubs, rocks and ivy. The churchyard is in two parts, connected by a charming bridge across the stream.

Saundersfoot (135045). Now given over almost entirely to the holiday industry, this is an attractive village which has seen much recent growth. Nowadays the glorious sandy beach and the safe bathing and sailing waters of the bay are the main attractions, but Saundersfoot first came to prominence as a coal exporting port. The inland coalmines were connected to the harbour by railway lines that ran through the village, and from 1829 onwards there were sailing vessels (and later on, steam vessels) coming in on every tide, and departing with holds full of top-quality anthracite

St. David's Cathedral, half hidden in the "valley of the roses" (Jan Gregson)

Tenby Harbour - departure point for Caldey

and also pig iron from the Stepaside iron works. Coal shipments ceased at the onset of the Second World War, and since that time the harbour has gradually been given over to use by pleasure craft. Traces of the area's industrial past are now difficult to find, but some of the old builsings of the old iron works can still be seen at Stepaside, and there are still a few traces of the Bonville's Court and other collieries. The tunnels which connect Saundersfoot, Coppet Hall and Wiseman's Bridge are the old tunnels used by the railway to Stepaside and Kilgetty The most attractive buildings in the area today are the parish church of Haroldston St. Issels, in a lovely sylvan setting not far from Coppet Hall, and the imposing Hean Castle on the hill to the north of Saundersfoot.

Slebech (033140). Most of Slebech parish is taken up with the Picton and Slebech estates. In the 12th century there was a Commandery of the Knights of St. John here, with the rights of sanctuary for criminals and refugees; the ruined chapel stands beside the 18th century Slebech Hall, and a service is held here once a year on the last Sunday in June. The new Slebech Church, which stands alongside the A40, dates from 1844.

Solva (805245). A favourite holiday resort, centred on a deep and very beautiful rocky creek which is flooded except at low tide. The name has a Viking origin, and means "sunny inlet". There is a great seafaring tradition here, and shipbuilding and coastal trading operations were in full swing until the coming of the railway to West Wales killed off most of the ship-borne trade. In 1773 Solva was the base for the assembly of the first Smalls lighthouse. The village is in two parts - Lower Solva is the place where holidaymakers congregate, with small-boat sailors conspicuous around the old quays and with many visitors enjoying the shops and Nectarium in the main street. Up the valley at Middle Mill there is a pretty hamlet with a woollen mill and an old corn mill now used as a shop and buttery.

Spittal (977230). An interesting Landsker village, more English than Welsh, just to the east of the A40 near Treffgarne. There is a simple bellcote church, a "rath" and an compact village layout including a village green. There was once a hospitium here (hence the name) probably used by pilgrims *en route* for St. David's. There are strip fields around the village revealing Norman influence. In the 1700's the village was used by the cattle drovers, and there was a thriving tannery. Now the village lies within Haverfordwest's "commuter belt", and there is much modern housing.

Stackpole (984964). A quiet and very beautiful corner of Pembrokeshire, centred on the old Stackpole Estate. Stackpole Court has been demolished, but the little village that remains is full of character. The Estate is now owned by the National Trust, and its renovated buildings are being put to good use. The church is at Stackpole Elidor, just over half a mile away. Nearby are deep wooded valleys, the Bosherston Lily Ponds, the charming little harbour of Stackpole Quay, and the remote and lovely sandy beach of Barafundle Bay.

Steynton (917077). Like a number of other settlements in the area, the village has a Norse name. There is a church with a tall tower, visible from miles around. There has been much recent development, and ribbon development has almost turned the village into a suburb of Milford.

Tenby (132004). The first and foremost of Pembrokeshire's holiday resorts, with a population well practised in the art of looking after visitors. The town is very old. There was a Welsh settlement here before the Normans arrived, but the castle (of which little remains) was part of the fortified town built in the twelfth century and strengthened in the thirteenth. The town walls are massive, and the parts that remain are still in a good state of repair. In Tudor and Stuart times the town was an important fishing and trading centre, and there were many rich merchants here; the Tudor Merchants House and Plantagenet House both date from the fifteenth century. From the middle of the eighteenth century the town became a popular health resort and many new houses were built above the two town beaches to accommodate the gentry. The main developer was Sir William Paxton, who built the sea-water baths at Laston House. Nowadays the harbour is the main focus of interest, full of pleasure boats during the summer and the departure point for the Caldey Island boats. St. Mary's Church, in the centre of the town, is the largest parish church in Wales, dating from the thirteenth century. Other notable buildings are St. Julian's fisherman's chapel, Tenby Museum on Castle Hill and St. Catherine's Fort on a little island approached on foot at low tide. There is much modern holiday development around Tenby, including a number of very large caravan sites.

Treffgarne (956236). The Welsh hero Owain Glyndwr was born here. The village is not very significant, with a rambling collection of houses and bungalows in the vicinity of a little bellcote church. Treffgarne Gorge is far more interesting - a natural routeway followed by road, rail and river. This deep cleft through the upland ridge of mid-Pembrokeshire was once a haunt of robbers (and wolves), and it has always been well-wooded. There are large stone quarries here, now abandoned. Above the gorge are the sentinel rocks of Maiden Castle and Lion Rock - among the oldest rocks in Pembrokeshire and reminiscent of the Dartmoor tors. At the northern end of the gorge is the tourist centre of Nant-y-Coy Mill.

West Williamston (035058). One of the great limestone quarrying centres of the past century. Look at the O.S. 1:50,000 map to obtain a vivid impression of the extent of the workings and of the "locks" used by barges to load up with limestone blocks and rubble. At the turn of the century the quarries employed 150 men, and limestone from here was used for the building of Pembroke Dockyard. Now the village has declined greatly, having lost its church, its pubs and its quarrymen. There is an Oiled Bird Centre in one of the farm buildings, managed by members of the West Wales Naturalists' Trust.

Wiston (023180). Manorial settlement founded by Wizo the Fleming early in the twelfth century. There was once a castle here with a motte crowned by a shell keep, but the whole castle site is now derelict. Opposite the castle site is a typical Little England church, extensively restored in 1864. On nearby Colby Moor, in the year 1645, Royalist Forces were routed by the Parliamentarians under Col. Rowland Laugharne.

Roch Castle, in ruins during the last century

Tenby Town Walls

Like other medieval towns, Tenby was protected by stout walls and a Norman castle. The castle has all but been destroyed by the passage of time, but the walls are well preserved. They were first built in the thirteenth century following the sacking of the town by Llewllyn ap Gruffydd. At this time virtually all of the buildings of the town would have been contained within the walls, and access was provided by at least four gates. In the later part of the fifteenth century the walls on the landward side of the town were strengthened and increased in height, and outside them a deep, wide ditch was excavated to provide extra defence. The only gatehouse to have survived to the present day is the South Gate, popularly known as "The Five Arches".

Richard
SYKES
Chartered Valuation Surveyors
AUCTIONEERS & ESTATE AGENTS

Dark Street
HAVERFORDWEST
Tel: (0437) 4463

Hill House
NARBERTH
Tel: (0834) 860260

FOR ALL YOUR PROPERTY REQUIREMENTS CONTACT US

Regular Thursday Auction Sales throughout the year of Antiques and Modern Items
500 – 1000 Lots every Sale
QUEENS HALL – NARBERTH
Worth a Visit when in Pembrokeshire
Enquire for date of our next Sale

THE GOOD BEACH GUIDE

There are beaches for all tastes in Pembrokeshire, ranging from the vast sandy expanse of Newgale to the little cove of Cwm-yr-Eglwys and from the crowded bustle of Saundersfoot to the isolation and peace of Aberrhigian.
In the following gazetteer there is space only for brief details about each beach; more information can be obtained from Tony Roberts' booklet called *The Beaches of Pembrokeshire*. The 40 or so beaches listed are all located by grid reference, and they are arranged in order from a starting-point at Amroth to a finishing-point at Poppit on the Teifi Estuary.

The South Coast

Amroth (170070). Extensive sandy beach backed by shingle banks. Groynes and other sea defences built in an attempt to reduce coastal erosion. Safe bathing. Occasional glimpses of the submerged forest following stormy spells. Car-parking reasonable, but crowded in summer. Refreshments and other facilities.

Wiseman's Bridge (147060). Sandy beach with some rocky areas. Shingle bank between beach and road. Some car-parking, but very crowded in summer. Within easy walking distance of Saundersfoot, across sands at low tide and through the old railway tunnels at high water. Safe bathing.

Saundersfoot (140050). Extensive sandy beaches to both sides of the harbour. The tide goes out a long way, and the beach can be muddy at low tide. The main beach is adjacent to the village and is very crowded in summer, but to the north, Coppit Hall beach may (or may not!) be less crowded, and to the south there are a number of little sandy coves between the harbour and Monkstone Point. The village, once a coal-exporting port, is now devoted to the holiday trade; refreshments and all necessary amenities are available. The harbour is a popular centre for sailing boats and other vessels. Sporting activities include wind-surfing, sailing, sub-aqua and fishing. Plenty of opportunities for boat trips.

Tenby North Beach (135006). Splendid sandy beach overlooked by steep cliffs and the northern part of the town. Easy access via steps from the town centre, and also from the harbour which is dry at low water. The beach is normally very crowded in fine weather, and bathing is safe at all states of the tide. All facilities - accommodation, playground, bowls, golf, deckchairs, cafés, ice cream, aqualung lessons, sailing and windsurfing lessons, and so on. Boat trips to Caldey, and fishing and other sightseeing trips from the harbour. Lifeboat station just round the corner. Like Saundersfoot, a real "resort beach". No car-parking adjacent to beach, but public car parks are a short walk away.

Tenby South Beach (126995). A wonderful sweep of firm sand stretching for a mile and a half from Giltar Point to Castle Beach. Safe bathing, and very sheltered from the prevailing south-westerlies. The beach is backed by high sand dunes called The Burrows, and Tenby Golf Course is nearby. The beach is excellent for children, and is heavily used by holidaymakers from the large caravan parks at Kiln Park and Penally. Car-parking and other facilities at Penally, reached by footpath across the dunes.

Lydstep Haven (093084). There is a private caravan settlement here in a very pretty wooded setting. The beach is wide and sandy, easily accessible from the coastal footpath or from the village. Charge for car-parking. Fine caves in the limestone cliffs, especially the Smugglers Cave at the western end of the headland. Old limestone quarries above the beach. Nature trail leaflet published by WWNT available locally.

Skrinkle Haven (080973). Open at long last following the reduction in the military presence at Manorbier Camp. Visit it while it's still peaceful! Famous for the junction between the Carboniferous Limestone and the Old Red Sandstone. Difficult access via a long flight of steps, but the beach itself is pleasant. Car-parking and easy access to picnic area on the clifftop nearby.

Manorbier Bay (057975). One of the loveliest beaches in Pembrokeshire, with its golden sand, its sand dunes and its castle and church in the background. Charge for car-parking; some parking on the roadside verge above the beach, but very crowded in summer. Facilities including shop in the village, ¼ mile from the beach. The castle and church are well worth visits.

Freshwater East (020976). A fine sandy beach, safe for bathing and well sheltered from the westerlies. The slopes above the beach are dotted with holiday homes, some beautiful but others revolting. A planner's nightmare; the National Park Authority dreams of a proper holiday development here, but progress is slow. Refreshments, car-parking and other facilities.

Barafundle Bay (992950). A beautiful beach flanked by limestone cliffs. Firm sand and safe bathing. No road access, so the beach is relatively uncrowded and unspoilt. No amenities. Access on the Coastal Path either from Stackpole Quay or from Broad Haven.

Broad Haven (978940). Referred to as "Broad Haven South" to distinguish it from the other Broad Haven on St. Bride's Bay. A fine sandy beach with limestone cliffs and rocks offshore.

Sand dunes, cliffs, and Bosherston Lily Pools just inland from the northern corner of the sands. Charge for car-parking, but the car park is spacious. Steps down to beach. No amenities, but café and inn at Bosherston.

Freshwater West (880000). A wide open beach with glorious sands in the north. In the south there is a wide and rough rocky area (fascinating to geologists and pebble hunters) around the headlands called Little Furzenip and Great Furzenip. Access to the south is prohibited, but the beach has good access from the car park in the dunes. Plenty of room for picnics and walks. *Do not bathe here*, even if you see surf-board enthusiasts sporting in the surf. There are quicksands, dangerous currents and undertows even when the sea looks calm.

A Llangwm fisherwoman pictured outside St. Mary's Church, Haverfordwest, in the late 1800's.

Milford Haven Area

West Angle Bay (853032). A small but very pleasant and safe sandy beach on the east side of the Haven entrance. A good viewing point for the oil tankers passing in and out. Good car par close to the beach, café, toilets. Nearby caravan site. Fascinating geological formations, especially in the little coves to the north of the main beach. Old brick-pit and brickworks near the café. Good views from the coastal footpath both to N and S.

Gelliswick Bay (888056). The innermost sandy beach on the Haven, but the sand is only revealed at low tide. Not a good beach for bathing, but used nevertheless by local people from the Milford - Hakin area. Also a popular sailing centre.

Dale (813056). A very sheltered beach facing east directly along the Haven. Not much sand, except at low water. Otherwise the beach is stony and not very comfortable. Nevertheless, a great place for the sailing fraternity. The village is very popular during the summer - café, pub, shop, boat chandlery, boat hire, sailing lessons. Out towards Dale Point is the Dale Fort Field Centre.

West Dale Bay (799059). A sandy beach backed by shingle and by crumbly cliffs made of Ice Age deposits. Access is by footpath only, from the field behind Dale Castle. Parking is a problem in summer - best to leave cars in Dale and walk the ¼ mile or so. Because this is a W-facing bay there can be heavy surf; be careful of the undertow when the tide is falling.

Marloes Sands (785074). According to the experts, the most beautiful beach in Pembrokeshire, with spacious golden sands and many stacks and rocky crags projecting through. The cliffs are geologically fascinating, with strata standing on end; many rock pools for the children to explore. Plenty of flotsam and jetsam; please don't add to it. Generally safe bathing, but there can be ferocious surf when the wind is SW. Access via Marloes to a large car park, but then there is a walk of ½ mile to the beach. Gateholm can be reached at low tide. No amenities, either on the beach or in the car park.

St. Bride's Bay

Musselwick Sands (785090). A remote, wide and sandy beach not far from Marloes. No access by car; visitors must walk from the Marloes - Martin's Haven road. But well worth the walk - solitude, good bathing and interesting cliffs. No amenities.

Little Haven (857130). Another of the favourite beaches of Pembrokeshire. The village, accessible by road only after steep descents from all directions, is most attractive - the houses, inns and guest houses are clustered on the valley floor around the head of the inlet. There is a good car park. The beach is firm and sandy, excellent for bathing at all states of the tide. A popular spot for boating, even if the beach is somewhat short of boat-parking space.

Broad Haven (860137). A splendid beach, open to the west but sheltered from the south-westerlies by the mass of the Dale Peninsula. The sand is firm and clean and easily accessible from the village. Excellent rock pools both to north and south. There is a large car park adjacent to the Pembrokeshire Countryside Unit and Youth Hostel. All necessary facilities here - shops, hotels, cafés, catravan parks etc. Much modern housing development - like Freshwater East this is planned as one of the "development areas" of the National Park.

Druidston Haven (860170). A fine sandy beach, reached either on the Coastal Footpath or by car along a minor road from Nolton or Broad Haven. No car-parking facilities, but often space on the roadside verges. Track down to the beach - not recommended for disabled visitors. The beach is backed by a mass of Ice Age deposits, and there are massive cliffs (which are dangerous and liable to rockfalls) both to north and south. No amenities. Safe bathing, but beware of currents at low tide.

Nolton Haven (859186). A good sandy beach contained between high cliffs, just to the south of the great bastion of Rickets Head. The road descends to the head of the inlet, making for easy access onto the beach. Good spacious car park. Shop, café and inn, although the village is about half a mile away to the SE. When bathing, beware of currents on a falling tide.

Newgale (850220). The most spacious sandy beach in Pembrokeshire, less wild than Freshwater West but nevertheless beautiful, with the cliffs of Dewisland sweeping away to the north and west. No matter how large the crowds using this beach, there is always room, especially at the southern end away from the caravan/camp site and away from the inn and shops. The Newgale pebble embankment is one of the natural wonders of Pembrokeshire, made up of both local and foreign stones swept up by the sea from glacial deposits on the floor of the bay. Generally safe bathing, but when there is heavy surf beware of a strong undertow and beware of the force of the breakers. A popular place for surfing and also for sand-yachting during the winter months.

Solva (800240). An immensely popular holiday spot, with the lower part of the village clustered at the head of a deep, narrow tidal inlet. Like the harbour of Lower Town Fishguard, this is the exit of an old glacial meltwater channel. The narrow ridge of The Gribin, which is surmounted by an Iron Age Fort, separates Solva Harbour from another deep valley. This latter valley has a sandy beach (The Gwadn) at its mouth. Inside the harbour itself there are some sandy areas when the tide is out - but much of the floor of the harbour is made of stones and mud. Solva is idyllic at high water, with a multitude of good diving points for confident swimmers. There are boats everywhere - sailing boats, rowing boats, canoes, and motor boats of all shapes and sizes. The ancient maritime tradition is in no danger of dying out. In the village there are good shops, inns, guest houses and assorted distractions. Fine cliff walking.

On Pembrokeshire's most famous Beach

Newgale Filling Station

and Camp Site

(NO CARAVANS)

Shell Petrol, Car Parts, Calor and Camping Gaz
Office for Camp Site – Car Park for Beach
Surf Boards and Deck Chairs for Hire
Also Maps, Books, Sunglasses, Sweets, etc.

Sands Café and Shop

Café with Sea Views
Shop with Ice-Cream, Drinks and Sweets
Beach Goods, Gifts and Groceries
Maps, Books, Magazines and Newspapers

P.J. and J.R. Gale *Telephone: St. Davids 721398*

Caerfai (760243). The closest beach to the city of St. David's. Reached by a steep path from the clifftop car park. The sand is firm and the bathing safe. Interesting cliffs with rock pools on both sides of the bay. The quarries on the clifftop provided some of the stone for St. David's Cathedral. On the promontory between Caerfai and Caerbwdi there is a magnificent Iron Age Fort.

Porth-clais (743240). This little creek, cutting into the plateau of the St. David's Peninsula, was once the harbour of St. David's. The ruined harbour wall, frequently patched up over the ages, probably dates from the 12th or 13th century. The creek is flooded at high tide and muddy and stony at low water. Not a bathing beach. Good car-parking at the head of the creek; interesting renovated lime-kilns and other examples of management cosmetics. Easy cliff walks to east and west - the cliff colours are surprisingly vivid.

Whitesands Bay (Porth-mawr) (733270). This is a splendid beach with a long stretch of firm sand, spectacular cliff scenery to the north and a fine backdrop of rocky crags in the shape of Carnllidi and Carnedd-lleithr. Sand dunes and golf-course; nearby youth hostel; large car park with café and shop. The beach is on the route between St. David's and the magical mysteries of St. David's Head. Little wonder that the beach is very crowded in the summer. Bathing is generally safe, but beware of dangerous currents at the north end of the beach. Also, beware of undertow when the surf is heavy. Lifeguards are on duty during the summer.

The North Coast

Abereiddi (797312). One of the favourite north coast beaches, easily accessible by car and with ample parking just above high water mark. Firm sand at low water; the sand is black and coarse, but quite clean! Safe bathing. Attractive cottages near the road; note also the ruined quarrymen's row which was once throbbing with life when the slate quarries were working. The Blue Lagoon is an abandoned quarry - now a safe anchorage for boats. The quarry was once connected to Porthgain by a little railway which ran along the side of the valley. Not surprisingly, this is a favourite spot with local artists.

Traethllyfn (802320). A fine beach, facing due west, accessible on foot from either Abereiddi or Porthgain. Access to the clifftop through Barry Island Farm on payment of a fee. Steep steps down to the beach; not for the faint-hearted. But the sand is firm, the bathing safe, and the cliff scenery and rock pools full of interest. Be careful that you are not cut off by the rising tide, and watch out for rock-falls beneath some of the cliff faces.

Porthgain (815327). There is a small sandy beach beside the harbour, and good bathing can be enjoyed at high tide. The little creek is dominated by industrial archeology - the harbour, the ruined stone-crushing plant and stone hoppers, the massive roofless engine shed, the old lime kiln, and much else besides. Good car-parking space, pub and café. A fascinating place for those interested in Pembrokeshire's industrial past. Old quarries to the west; excellent cliff walks to the east.

Abercastle (852337). This little creek opening onto the north coast has a sandy beach and is a favourite with many holidaymakers. Once a port with a busy coastal trade; the old granary on the east side of the cove is a reminder of long-gone seafaring days. A cluster of holiday cottages; not much life here during the winter. No amenities except for toilets and small car park. Popular for sailing, sub-aqua, and canoeing. Reasonable access for boats onto the beach.

Abermawr (883347). A fine sandy beach except when winter storms have stripped away the sand. Massive pebble beach which dams back the small stream in the valley. This valley, which looks too large for such a stream, was once the exit route for the Western Cleddau river. The ice of the last glaciation changed all that. The submerged forest is sometimes visible at low water. Thick glacial and periglacial deposits at the northern end of the beach; note how these deposits have been eroded away by the sea, carrying away the old roadway as they have collapsed. No amenities, but the beach is quite popular nevertheless; car-parking on the roadside verge only, and definitely **not** in the turning bay.

Goodwick (Parrog) (950380). The beach, which fronts Goodwick Moor, is extremely well sheltered except when the wind is in the north-east. Safe and sandy, although shingly at high tide. A good bathing beach. Boat park and slipway make this a popular beach for small-boat sailors. Amenities good, including a spacious car park, café, petrol stations, toilets. A fine beach for sea angling (off the breakwaters) and for water sports such as canoeing, water skiing, sub-aqua, etc. The Rosslare ferries leave from Fishguard Harbour, out beyond the beach.

Lower Fishguard (960373). Not a good bathing beach (too muddy and stony), but one of the prettiest places in Pembrokeshire, with the cottages of Lower Town clustered in the south-eastern corner of the harbour. Sailing boats and motor-boats galore; this is a place with a nautical flavour. Boat trips during the summer - also landings of fresh fish and shellfish. Good amenities - toilets, cafés, shops etc. Swimming off the rocks at high tide or beneath the Old Fort (for confident swimmers only) at most states of the tide.

Pwllgwaelod (004399). The western beach of Dinas Island. Grey sand; safe bathing. Good car-parking space here, just above high water mark. A pleasant beach for water sports too, although the road access for cars with trailers is not good. Can be very crowded during the summer. Interesting cliffs and cliff walking around Dinas Island. Notice how much more exposed the cliff scenery is here than around Cwm-yr-Eglwys on the lee side. Popular pub on the beach.

Cwm-yr-Eglwys (015400). One of Pembrokeshire's prettiest coves. Sandy beach at most states of the tide; safe for bathing. Slipway for small boats, car park, toilets. There is a path along the cwm to Pwllgwaelod, and the Dinas Island path climbs away to the north. There is a Mediterranean feel about the cove, with its low rock cliffs, its calm sea, its cottages clinging to the slopes above the beach, and its lush vegetation. The ruined church set in its ancient churchyard provides added interest.

Aberfforest (026397). A small cove below Fforest Farm, very sheltered from the W and SW, and with safe bathing. Sand at low water; shingle higher up the beach. No vehicular access; can be approached only on foot from the main road or along the Coastal Footpath. No amenities.

Aberrhigian (032397). This little cove, similar to Aberfforest, is totally unspoilt. Not a single building in sight. The beach is safe, and sandy at low water. Very sheltered. Lovely grassy banks behind the beach; you may have to share the territory with grazing cows while you have your picnic. One of the most idyllic spots on the north Pembrokeshire coast. Approached from the main road via a wooded valley; cars can be parked on the verge above the first gate, followed by a walk of about ¼ mile. Otherwise, approach on foot along the Coastal Footpath from Parrog. The bays along this stretch of coast are fascinating, with many abandoned Sea Quarries which once provided slate for local buildings.

Parrog (Newport) (050397). The beach here is part of the Nevern estuary, sandy at low tide but stony when the tide is up. Muddy sand along the river and upstream of the Boat Club. Generally safe for bathing at high water, but dangerous currents along the river on an ebb tide. There is safer bathing at Cwm, a little cove at the eastern end of Parrog. Very easy access - large car park above the beach, slipway for getting sailing boats into the water. Good safe moorings inside the old trading quays. Café, boat club, shops, restaurant and guest house, toilets near car park. Touring caravan sites and camping sites nearby. There is a pleasant walk along a good path towards Cat Rock and beyond.

Traeth Mawr (Newport) (053405). This is Newport's "big beach" - the finest beach on the north Pembrokeshire coast. Firm, extensive sands sweeping out to a bar across the Nevern estuary; sand dunes (now subject to protection measures) behind the beach. Safe bathing at all states of the tide, although heavy surf if the wind is in the north-west. Large car park next to the beach; toilets; shop and surf lifesaving clubhouse. Cars are allowed onto the beach, much to the disgust of some - but the beach is large enough to take quite a fleet of vehicles, and the southern part is now a prohibited zone for cars. Adjoining 9-hole golf-course in one of the most attractive locations in Pembrokeshire. Wonderful cliff walks to the north around Morfa Head.

Poppit Sands (155486). Located at the mouth of the Teifi, there is a fine extensive sandy beach. Sand underfoot at all states of the tide. Spacious car park, café and shop, toilets. Easy access for disabled people. Bathing generally safe, but there are dangerous currents around the deep water channel on the ebb or if the river is in flood. There are lifeguards on duty here - bathe only in accordance with their advice. Youth hostel nearby, and the Coastal Footpath starts from the road above the estuary.

Richards Bros

BRITISH & CONTINENTAL TOUR OPERATORS

Regular holiday tours to most British & European destinations telephone now for a brochure.
Volvo Highliner Executive Coaches for hire with T.V., Video, Stereo, Toilet, Reclining Seats, Tables & Air Suspension.

FOR YOUR COACH TOUR
OR PRIVATE HIRE
Try us next time

DAILY SERVICES OPERATED BETWEEN HAVERFORDWEST, FISHGUARD, NEWPORT, CARDIGAN, ABERPORTH,TRESAITH, ST. DAVIDS, NEWGALE, SOLVA AND GOODWICK.

TIMETABLES, BRITISH AND CONTINENTAL HOLIDAY BROCHURES AVAILABLE

RICHARDS BROS, MOYLGROVE GARAGE, CARDIGAN, DYFED

TELEPHONES: CARDIGAN 613756; NEWPORT 820751; ST. DAVIDS 721428.
AFTER HOURS: CARDIGAN 612920; NEWPORT 820678 and 820324. TELEX: 48554

Solva Harbour (Betsy Temple).

BOOKSTALL

This little book has no space for an "in depth" look at Pembrokeshire. However, if you feel that some of the topics touched upon deserve further investigation you will be well advised to visit the local bookshops and information centres, where a wide range of books and pamphlets about the region are to be found. If you have difficulty in finding specific texts, the libraries listed on page 14 may well be able to help you.

Things to read

Barrett, J.H. *The Pembrokeshire Coast Path* (London, 1974)

Bassett, M.G. *Geological Excursions in Dyfed, S.W. Wales* (Cardiff, 1982)

Chamberlain, D.G. *Welsh Nicknames* (Caernarfon, 1981)

Bennett, T. *Welsh Shipwrecks* (Vols. 1, 2 and 3) (Haverfordwest, 1981)

Bielski, A. *Tales and Traditions of Old Tenby* (Tenby, 1981)

Charles, B.G. *George Owen of Henllys* (Aberystwyth, 1973)

Condry, W.M. *The Natural History of Wales* (London, 1981)

Davies, M. *The Story of Tenby* (Tenby, 1979)

Davies, M. *Pembrokeshire Children in History* (Llandysul, 1983)

Davies, T.A.W. *Plants of Pembrokeshire* (Haverfordwest, 1970)

Ellis-Gruffydd, I.D. *Rocks and Landforms of the Pembrokeshire Coast National Park* (Newport, 1977)

Ellis-Gruffydd, I.D. *Coastal Scenery of the Pembrokeshire Coast National Park* (Newport, 1977)

Evans, R.O. and John, B.S. *The Pembrokeshire Landscape* (Tenby, 1973)

Gallie, M. *Little England's Other Half* (Abercastle, 1974)

Goddard, T. *Pembrokeshire Shipwrecks* (Llandybie, 1983)

Harris, P.V. *Pembrokeshire Place-Names and Dialect* (Tenby, 1974)

Hearn, P. *The Last Invasion of Britain* (Fishguard, 1980)

Howells, B.E. *Pembrokeshire Life 1572-1843* (Haverfordwest, 1972)

Howells, R. *The Sounds Between* (Tenby, 1976)

Howells, R. *Old Saundersfoot* (Llandysul, 1977)

Howells, R. *Total Community* (Tenby, 1975)

James, D.W. *St. David's and Dewisland - a social history* (Cardiff, 1981)

Jennett, S. *South-West Wales* (London, 1967)

John, B.S. *Ports and Harbours of Pembrokeshire* (Abercastle, 1974)

John, B.S. *Scenery of Dyfed* (Newport, 1976)

John, B.S. *The Geology of Pembrokeshire* (Abercastle, 1979)

John, B.S. *Honey Harfat - a Haverfordwest Miscellany* (Newport, 1979)

John, B.S. (ed.) *Wildlife in Dyfed* (Haverfordwest, 1970)

John, B.S. *Milford Haven Waterway* (Newport, 1981)

John, B.S. *Presely Hills* (Newport, 1981)

John, B.S. *Pembrokeshire* (new edition) (Newport, 1984)

Jones, L. *Schoolin's Log* (London, 1980)

Knights, P. *Birds of the Pembrokeshire Coast* (Newport, 1979)

Kruys, I. *Butterflies of Pembrokeshire* (Newport, 1981)

Lewis, E.T. *Mynachlogddu - a Historical Survey* (Mynachlogddu, 1969)

Lewis, E.T. *North of the Hills* (Mynachlogddu, 1972)

Lockley, R. *The Island* (London, 1969)

Miles, D. *Pembrokeshire Coast National Park* (National Park Guide No. 10) (London, 1973)

Miles, D. *A Pembrokeshire Anthology* (Llandybie, 1983)

Morris, J.P. *The North Pembroke and Fishguard Railway* (Lingfield, 1969)

Morris, J.P. *The Railways of Pembrokeshire* (Tenby, 1981)

Mortlock, C. *Rock Climbing in Pembrokeshire* (Tenby, 1974)

Owen, G. *Description of Pembrokeshire* (ed. H. Owen) (original 1603; London, 1906)
Pembrokeshire Coast National Park Authority *Handbook* (Haverfordwest, 1983)
Price, M.R.C. *Industrial Saundersfoot* (Llandysul, 1982)
Pugh, R.J. and Holiday, F.W. *The Dyfed Enigma* (London, 1981)
Rees, V. *South-West Wales* (Shell Guide) (London, 1976)
Roberts, A. *See the Best of Pembrokeshire* (Abercastle, 1981)
Roberts, A. *The Best Walks in Pembrokeshire* (Abercastle, 1977)
Roberts, A. *The Beaches of Pembrokeshire* (Abercastle, 1973)
Saunders, D. *A Brief Guide to the Birds of Pembrokeshire* (Tenby, 1975)
Scott, V. *Inferno 1940* (Haverfordwest, 1980)
Stark, P. *Walking the Pembrokeshire Coast Path* (Tenby, 1973)
Titchmarsh, P. *The Pembrokeshire Coast by Car* (Norwich, 1974)
Warburton, F.W. *The History of Solva* (London, 1944)
Williams, D. *The Rebecca Riots* (Cardiff, 1955)

Some recent Publications

Gibson, P. *The Visitor's Guide to South and West Wales* (Ashbourne, 1985)
John, B.S. *The Ancient Game of Cnapan* (Newport, 1985)
John, B.S. *Pembrokeshire Crafts and Cottage Craft Producers* (Newport, 1985)
Jones, A. *Welsh Capels* (Cardiff, 1984)
Malloy, P. *And They Blessed Rebecca* (Llandysul, 1984)
Morgan, G. (ed). *Dyfed County Handbook* (Carmarthen, 1986)
Pembrokeshire Regional Library. *Crafts in Pembrokeshire* (Carmarthen, 1984)
Saunders, D. *The Nature of West Wales* (Buckingham, 1986)
Shepherd, A. *A Visitor's Guide to Tenby and South Pembrokeshire* (Tenby, 1985)
Worsley, R. *Open Secrets* (Llandysul, 1986)

WALES' FINEST
STANDARD GAUGE
PRESERVED LINE

Train Rides – Steam Trains
Riverside Picnic Area
Souvenirs – Buffet
Fare allows unlimited travel
on day of issue

NEW EXTENSION OPEN MID 1986

OPEN:

Bank Holiday Weekends
Sundays in June and September
Weekends in July
Also July 1st, 2nd, 3rd until 3 p.m.
Then every day except
Thursday and Friday from
21st July until 31st August
inclusive.

Situated just North of Carmarthen on the A484 Cardigan and Newcastle Emlyn Road

BRONWYDD ARMS STATION
NEAR CARMARTHEN — DYFED

ADULTS £1.30
OAP/CHILD £ .30
SPECIAL FAMILY RATES
AND PARTY DISCOUNTS

Whitesands Bay and the rocky crag of Carnllidi

Tenby Harbour on a summer day

WHERE TO BUY YOUR PEMBROKESHIRE BOOKS

THE BOOKMARK

1 Quay Street, Haverfordwest
for
Books of interest, Maps,
Newspapers, Greeting Cards,
View cards and stationery
requirements

Open Mon. to Sat. 8.30 to 5.30
Telephone: 0437 - 2633

Members of the Booksellers Association

For books of local interest

A L L E N ' S

of Narberth

22 High Street, Narberth
Booksellers and Stationers. Book Tokens.
Telephone: Narberth 860276

THE ST. DAVIDS BOOKSHOP
SIOP LYFRAU TYDDEWI

BOOKSELLER & PUBLISHER

A wide range of books available from leading publishers • Local guidebooks • Welsh books and books of Welsh interest • O.S. Maps • • Book Tokens • Children's books • • Records • Greetings and birthday cards • • Pictures and prints • H.M.S.O. publications •

The Pebbles, St. Davids (nr. to Cathedral Gateway) Tel: St. Davids (0437) 720480

While in Haverfordwest visit

VICTORIA BOOKSHOP

for
● Local Guides ● Maps ● Books
● Newspapers ● Postcards
● Greeting Cards ● Stationery

Victoria Bookshop, 5 Victoria Place
Castle Square, Haverfordwest
Telephone: (0437) 2750

SHAW'S

V.S. and P.L. NEWSAGENTS
87 Charles Street, Milford Haven
Telephone: Milford Haven 2156
Open: 6.30 a.m. to 5.30 p.m.
six days a week

Newspapers, Magazines,
Paperbacks, Local Guide Books
Cards, Stationery, Confectionery

Pembrokeshire Bookshops

Most of the titles listed on pages 113-114 are still in print, and can be obtained from any of the bookshops listed below. The Pembrokeshire bookshops are all small establishments whose proprietors have a good knowledge of the local book scene and who give excellent personal service. So - support your nearest bookshop!

Allens of Narberth, 22 High Street, Narberth
Bookmark (Rex Hurst), 1 Quay Street, Haverfordwest
The Bookshop (Shirley Daniel), 34 Market Street, Haverfordwest
The Bookshop (Lewis Dodd), Market Street, Newport
Flyleaf Bookshop, 39 Charles Street, Milford Haven
Number One (Bob Starmore), Market Square, Fishguard
Pembroke Bookshop, 73 Main Street, Pembroke
Perowne's Bookshop (John Perowne), The Strand, Saundersfoot
Seaways Bookshop (Brian Henshall), West Street, Fishguard
Tenby Bookshop, Jubilee House, Tudor Square, Tenby
Victoria Bookshop (Marley Davies), 5 Victoria Place, Haverfordwest
St. David's Bookshop (Christopher Taylor), The Pebbles, St. David's
Olive Leaf Bookshop, 133, Charles Street, Milford Haven

In addition, good selections of local books are stocked in W.H. Smith's branches in Tenby, Haverfordwest, Pembroke Dock and Cardigan. Many newsagents stock a small range of local titles, and the tourist information centres sell National Park publications and a number of other titles, mostly relating to the National Park itself. Other retail outlets include the WWTNC Shop in Market Street, Haverfordwest; Cardigan Wildlife Park; Manor House Wildlife and Leisure Park; Kiln Park Holiday Centre, Tenby; Scolton Manor Museum, near Haverfordwest; and Lockley Lodge, Martin's Haven, near Marloes.

DID YOU KNOW ...

that around 1864 Saundersfoot Harbour was exporting up to 4,000 tons of pig iron annually from the Stepaside Iron Works?

that the "last invasion of Britain", by a French expeditionary force, took place on the Pen Caer coast near Fishguard in 1797?

that there was once a tin-plate works at Castell Malgwyn, near Llechryd in the Teifi Valley?

that Haverfordwest was the home of Llewellin's Churnworks, one of the most famous factories in the world for the manufacture of butter-churns in the nineteenth century?

that about one hundred years ago the little slate-quarrying village of Rosebush in the Presely Hills was being developed as a spa and tourist resort?

that about 15,000 years ago the wild animals roaming about the Pembrokeshire countryside included mammoth, giant deer, woolly rhinoceros, wolves and cave lions?

that in spite of Pembrokeshire's reputation as a slate-quarrying area most of the cottages of the 1700's and 1800's had thatched roofs?

WELSH WATER

SOUTH WESTERN DIVISION

Llys-y-Fran Reservoir Country Park

11 Miles NE of Haverfordwest

Fishing - Boating - Walking - Bird Watching
Cafeteria - Picnic Area

Fishing Permits obtainable from the Cafeteria.
Reduced Rates for O.A.P's. and Juveniles

Further information available from the Ranger on Site
or
Telephone: Maenclochog (09913) 273

Celtic Crosses

The great Celtic crosses of Pembrokeshire are perhaps the Christian equivalents of the prehistoric standing stones that were put up as monuments or sacred symbols. Only three great stone crosses have survived - at Nevern, Carew and Penally. They all belong in date to the tenth or eleventh century. The Nevern cross, which stands 13 feet high, may be seen in St. Brynach's churchyard not far from the church door. It is a "wheel-headed cross", ornately carved with Celtic-style interlacements, and so-called key and fret designs. The Penally Cross, now inside the church, has interesting vine-scrolls and interlaced animal motifs. The Carew Cross is a royal memorial, currently located in a dangerous position alongside the road near the entrance to Carew Castle but shortly to be removed to a safer site.

DID YOU KNOW ...

that Cardigan Island has a flock of Soay Sheep similar to those kept by Viking settlers in Scotland and Ireland in the period 800-1100AD?

that once upon a time King Arthur saw the Sword Excalibur rising from the waters of Bosherston Lily Ponds?

that south-western Pembrokeshire has become known among UFO-watchers as "The Welsh Triangle" as a result of many sightings of UFO's and other unexplained phenomena in the area round 1974-1977?

that the River Cleddau once had its own particular type of coracle, made with a squared-off bow and flat bottom?

that 200 years ago furze mills were quite common in Pembrokeshire, producing chopped gorse for animal feed?

OLD CUSTOMS

The Pembrokeshire Gwylnos
An extraordinary custom connected with the **Gwylnos** *or "Watch-night" was widely practised in Pembrokeshire in the eighteenth and nineteenth centuries. Especially in the Welsh-speaking districts of north Pembrokeshire it was the custom, following a death in the family, for a watch to be kept over the corpse every night until the funeral took place. Friends and neighbours would take it in turn to sit in the candle-lit room with the coffin. On the night before the funeral large numbers of men would call at the house. The corpse would be taken from the coffin, wrapped in a long white shroud and then tied with stout ropes. It would then be taken to the immense wide fireplace (the* **simle fawr)** *which was characteristic of Pembrokeshire houses and cottages at this time. A number of men would set up ladders against the outside of the house and clamber over the roof to the top of the chimney stack. Once in position, one end of the rope would be passed up the chimney to them by means of a long pole, and the men would haul the corpse up to the top of the chimney. Then, slowly but surely, the corpse would be lowered again and replaced in the coffin. The origins of this custom are very obscure, but in early times it may have been intended to ensure that the dead person's spirit left the house entirely in the possession of the living. The* **Gwylnos** *has long since died out, but it was still practised in the Solva district around 1850-1860.*

The Tenby Plygain Service
During the eighteenth century the people of Tenby kept alive a number of very old Christmas traditions which have since faded away. Late on Christmas Eve and in the early hours of Christmas Day the young people of the town held parties and made a special type of treacle toffee. Then, at 4 a.m., the young men called on the Rector and escorted him to St. Mary's Church in a torchlight procession. The early morning service was attended by crowds of church and chapel people together, and every member of the congregation took a lighted candle. Some of these were placed on the communion table, pulpit and window sills; other coloured candles were kept in the pews by those who wished to read the service. There were cards, traditional prayers and also new prayers written in a special metre by local poets. Some of the latter were too long for comfort. When the service ended candles were extinguished, blazing torches were lit, and the procession returned the Rector to the Rectory with the church bells ringing out the Christmas message over the dark town. The Welsh word for this service was **Plygain**, *which means "the morning light'. The* **Plygain** *carol services which still take place at Christmas in the Welsh-speaking districts have lost nearly all of their traditional trappings.*

Twelfth Night
On Twelfth Night a number of ancient customs were practised by Pembrokeshire people well within living memory. One of these was the revelry associated with the wassail bowl. This pottery bowl, which was a prized possession and often very elaborate in shape, was filled with ale or some other drink and carried around from house to house in a form of seasonal greeting. Those who drank from the bowl were expected to pay for the privilege, and a special wassail song was sung by the visitors.
Another custom was the bearing of the **Mari Lwyd**, *a grotesque horse's head made by draping a white sheet over a horse's skull and decorating it with button eyes, with gloves for ears. A man would stand beneath the sheet, moving the horse's head and uttering fearsome noises. This appirition would be carried around from house to house, with the horse's head pushed against the windows of unsuspecting neighbours who were sometimes absolutely terrified. The origins of this somewhat grotesque custom are lost in mystery.*

St. Govan's Chapel.

HAVE A DAY OUT

IN STYLE

WITH

SEALINK BRITISH FERRIES

Fishguard to Rosslare

Long Day Return (same as half day)

Licensed Bar and Restaurant on Board

On a Full Day excursion you can visit Wexford, Waterford or Dublin and Special Coach Tours are available from Rosslare on Tuesday/Wednesday/Thursday to include sightseeing, shopping and free evening entertainment. (Minimum of 10 people.)

Two FREE Excursion Tickets when you organise a group of 12 or more adults on a Day Trip booked in advance.

Bookings and Enquiries to:–
Fishguard (0348) 872881, your local Travel Agent or British Rail Station.

CHANGING FOR THE BETTER – FULL SPEED AHEAD

Welsh Nicknames

In Pembrokeshire there are too many Evanses, Joneses, Hugheses, Williamses and Thomases. It is not surprising, therefore, that nicknames have to be used to distinguish one person from another. The tradition of using nicknames is, of course, very old and such names are by no means restricted to those with the commonest surnames. Here are a few that might prove amusing:–

Evans the Death was (of course) a local undertaker.

Dai Loco was an engine driver.

Barry Central Eating had one tooth in the centre of his mouth.

Georgie One Ball had suffered an unfortunate accident.

Dai Eighteen Months had one complete ear and one half ear.

Will Population was the father of 13 children.

Davy Seven Waistcoats was always well dressed for the winter weather.

Dai Mikado once sang a part in a Gilbert & Sullivan opera.

Jack the Bomb was an early member of the CND.

Willie Bingo once had the misfortune to open a new bingo hall.

Dai Quiet Wedding is reputed to have worn gym shoes on the occasion of his marriage.

Dai Upper Crust is a local baker who once shook hands with a member of the royal family.

Horizontal Harry was a boxer who never made the grade.

Mrs. Dai Double Yolk was an egg merchant's wife who gave birth to twins.

Ned Bakerloo once lost his way on the London underground.

Toni Titanic weighed 20 stones.

Jones the Filth was a very respectable God-fearing newsagent whose wholesaler once sent him - in error - a parcel of girlie magazines.

Dai Quiet Wedding

Barry Central Eating

Jones the Filth

Early summer in Abereiddi Bay

BRUNEL QUAY HOTEL

Picton Road, Neyland, Pembrokeshire

Telephone: Neyland 600339

Ours is a small family-run Hotel, just 5 minutes' walk from the Marina.

We have a relaxing Lounge Bar where you can either have a Bar Meal or just a friendly drink.

There is a comfortable Dining Room which offers an extensive à la carte Menu with a range of 45 different Wines and Champagnes.

We have nine Bedrooms, most with shower and wash hand basin, and all with fully remote control colour television.

From Easter onwards we offer three course Family Lunches.

Your Hosts: David and Sheila Loosmore.

PEMBROKESHIRE TALES

Cantre'r Gwaelod
The north coast of Pembrokeshire once marked the southern margin of Cantre'r Gwaelod (Bottom Hundred) at a time when sea-level was lower than it is today. Much of the land now submerged beneath the murky waters of Cardigan Bay was fertile and beautiful, with 16 wealthy fortified towns and a busy and contented population. The land was protected from the sea by a great embankment and sluices, which were looked after by Seithennin, "one of the three immortal drunkards of Britain". One day, reputedly in 520 A.D., the Lord of Cantre'r Gwaelod, one Gwyddno Garanhir, was holding a great banquet for his nobles. Seithennin, having had a few too many, forgot to close the sluice gates as the tide rose. The sea breached the defences and rose remorselessly, flooding the whole of the lowland hundred and causing the death of most of the population by drowning. Some people escaped to North Wales, but Cantre'r Gwaelod was never reclaimed from the sea. Those who live along the present coastline will tell you that out at sea, when the water is clear and the weather calm, you can still see the ruined buildings on the sea floor. And if you listen carefully, you can still hear the church bells sounding faintly beneath the dark waters ....

Carew Cheriton Church

The Monkton Viking and the Ghostly Nun
Around the year 1930 the village of Monkton was vistited by a tall young man from Stockholm with the name of Nordin. He was a medical student. On a visit to the Vicar he related that in a previous incarnation he had been born in Monkton of Viking parents, more than 1,000 years earlier. The Vicar took Mr. Nordin to the top of the church tower, where the young man pointed out the locations of ancient walls which nobody in the neighbourhood knew about. On investigation, the Vicar later discovered these old walls. The young man also recognized the Old Hall at Monkton, told the Vicar where and how it had been altered over the years, and recalled that in his previous life it had been a nunnery. The Vicar had not previously been aware of this, but it helped him to explain a number of strange events in the Old Hall (then used as a vicarage) including a heavy knocking on his bedroom door every morning at four o'clock and various apparitions of a female figure dressed in long robe. The Vicar conjectured that the ghostly happenings in the vicarage involved an unhappy nun who had died while working on some penance for a sin she had committed.

The Phantom Funeral at Penally
There are many tales in Pembrokeshire concerning fetches or phantom funerals which were always held to be portents of real events. One such tale concerns Holloway Farm near Penally. On a winter's evening an employee of the vicar of Penally saw a large phantom funeral procession near Holloway Farm, and he recognized several neighbours among the mourners. The Vicar laughed at the man when told about this, and showed even greater scepticism when told that the phantom funeral had left the road, passing over a hedge bank into an adjacent field. The man showed the Vicar exactly where this had occurred, but there was no sign of trampling or any other disturbance. Shortly after this Mr. Williams, the tenant of Holloway Farm, died. On its way to the church the funeral party found the narrow lane blocked by snow, and the coffin was carried over the hedge bank at precisely the spot crossed by the phantom funeral some days earlier.

Gruffydd and the Invisible Islands
*Long ago there were green fertile islands out at sea beyond the Pembrokeshire coast, populated by the Fairy Folk (***Tylwyth Teg*** in Welsh). The strange thing about these islands was that sometimes they could be seen and sometimes not, even when the weather was clear and the sunlight bright. Once upon a time Gruffydd ab Einon was standing in St. David's churchyard when he saw the green islands out to sea. He ran down to the shore and put to sea in his boat but found that the islands had disappeared. The same thing*

happened a second time, but on the third occasion he took with him the piece of turf on which he had been standing in the churchyard, and the islands remained in view. This time he landed safely, to be welcomed by the fairy folk and to be shown their many wonderful treasures. On enquiring, Gruffydd was told that there were strange herbs on the islands which rendered them invisible, and that these herbs grew elsewhere only in St. David's churchyard and one square yard of turf somewhere in the old hundred of Cemais. Only by standing on the right place and by carrying a piece of the special turf with one is it possible to find the islands and set foot on them. Apparently Gruffydd continued to visit the islands for many years, becoming a good friend of the fairy folk and becoming very wealthy into the bargain. Undoubtedly, the islands are still there, visible only to those who stand on the right spot . . . .

PEMBROKESHIRE STORIES - STRANGE BEASTS

The Flying Snake of St. Edren's
It is said there was once a flying snake or Gwiber in the tower of lonely St. Edren's Church, built on the site of an ancient pagan burial ground. The snake is said to have flown from the tower to Grinston, where it lives on marshy ground. At night it coils up in the bottom of Grinston well, much to the consternation of nocturnal water-carriers.

The Trellyffant Toads
There is a strange story connected with the farm of Trellyffant, not far from Nevern. Once upon a time a young man called Cecil Longlegs fell ill, and was persecuted by a plague of toads. His friends killed as many as they could, but the toads simply increased in number at a frightening rate. At last, exhausted by their efforts, Cecil's friends decided to haul him up in a large bag into a high tree which they reckoned would be out of the reach of the toads. But Cecil could not escape from the pestilence; thousands and thousands of toads climbed up the tree, found their way into the bag and consumed the poor man until nothing was left but his white bones.

The Water Horse
The **Ceffyl Dwr** *was a small but beautiful horse which tempted unwary travellers to ride but which had a habit of suddenly galloping off towards the water, throwing off its riders in the process. Only ministers of religion were permitted an easy and safe ride. Once upon a time a water horse was seen in St. Bride's Bay after a fierce storm, and it was caught by a local farmer. The farmer caught the horse and used it uneventfully for several weeks, harnessed to its plough. One day, however, the horse suddenly rushed off towards the sea, dragging plough and ploughman with it until it entered the water and disappeared beneath the waves.*

LOCAL BOY MAKES GOOD

Henry Tudor, a local lad born in Pembroke Castle in the year 1457, did very well for himself. After a period of exile in France he returned to Pembrokeshire, marched with a Welsh army to Bosworth Field, and after the death of Richard III became Henry VII, the founder of the Tudor dynasty.

General Sir Thomas Picton was a Pembrokeshire man of many talents. Most of his career was spent in the army, and in the Napoleonic Wars he became the Duke of Wellington's right-hand man. When he was killed in the Battle of Waterloo in 1815 he was Wellington's second in command, a brilliant soldier much loved by his troops.

George Owen of Henllys, (1552-1613) was a north Pembrokeshire squire who was a good deal larger than life. He wrote the famous *Description of Pembrokeshire*, one of the most detailed and valuable accounts of Elizabethan Wales. But it is not widely known that Owen was one of the world's earliest amateur geologists who described in great detail some of the geological features of his home area.

Augustus John, the artist, was born in Tenby in 1878. At the time his parents were living in Haverfordwest, and it was in the county town that he spent the first six years of his childhood. Later the family moved to Tenby following the death of Augustus' mother.

Saint David was born under mysterious circumstances at St. Non's on the south coast of St. David's Peninsula. After a holy life as a missionary, priest and bishop, he was canonized and is now the patron saint of Wales. Thus he was a local boy who made *very* good.

Gerald the Welshman was born in Manorbier in 1146, and became one of the most famous men of his generation. He became an eminent cleric and wrote numerous books about Wales. He also travelled widely. Although he set his heart on becoming Bishop of St. David's, political intrigues prevented him from attaining this high office. He died in 1223.

"Don't worry about me — I'm just a figment of your imagination."

The Wiston Basilisk
Once upon a time a basilisk lived in a hide on a hillside near Wiston. It was a terrible beast, only a foot or two long, but with black and yellow skin, poisonous breath and eyes both in the front and back of its head. Furthermore, it could kill simply by looking at a human being. On the other hand, if anyone could look at the basilisk without first being seen, the beast would die. Several centuries ago there was a dispute between claimants to the Wiston estate, and it was agreed that the estate should go to the person who could kill the basilisk by looking at it while remaining invisible. After several claimants had tried unsuccessfully to outwit the basilisk, signing their own death warrants in the process, one bright young man climbed into a barrel and rolled down the hillside past the beast's lair. Peeping out through the bung-hole, he shouted "Ha! Bold Basilisk, I can see you but you can't see me!" In this way the basilisk was killed, and the bright young man became the owner of the Wiston estate.

King Arthur and the Monstrous Boar
One of the ancient stories related in **The Mabinogion** *concerns a heroic running battle between King Arthur and his knights and a Monstrous Boar called Twrch Trwyth. The unwitting cause of all the trouble was a young prince called Kilhwch, who was madly in love with a young lady called Olwen, whom he had never met. The girl's father was a wicked giant called Yspaddaden Penkawr, who set all suitors an assortment of seemingly impossible tasks in order to win her hand in marriage. Anyway, to cut a long story short, King Arthur had agreed to help this young prince in the task of stealing a comb, razor and scissors from between the ears of the great boar, who was a bad-tempered beast in view of the fact that he had once been a wicked Irish King. (And being a wicked Irish King was much more fun than being a boar with assorted strange objects stuck in between his ears.) When King Arthur travelled to Ireland to ask politely for the comb, razor and scissors Twrch Trwyth refused to speak to him, let alone make him a present of the desired objects, and instead he swam across to Wales, accompanied by seven young ferocious boars, to ravage Arthur's teritory. The boars landed at Porth-clais near St. David's and laid waste the districts around Milford Haven before Arthur and his knights caught up with them and pursued them to the Presely Hills. They fought one battle in the Nevern Valley and then another great and bloody battle in Cwm Cerwyn, the deep depression beneath the summit of Presely. Here four of Arthur's knights were killed. Turning at bay a second time the beast slew four more knights and was wounded himself, while several of the young boars were also killed. The chase continued to Llandissilio, then into Cardiganshire, then all over South Wales, with many local people falling victim to the boars and with four more knights slain. At last only Twrch was left. He was forced to swim out into the Severn estuary, where Arthur managed to grab the razor and scissors from between his ears. The comb was not obtained until the chase reached Cornwall, and then the great boar leaped into the sea and was never seen again. Then, armed with the razor, scissors and comb, Arthur cut Kilhwch's hair and helped him to kill the savage giant called Yspaddaden Penkawr (who was, you may recall, Olwen's dad), thereby enabling the handsome prince and the beautiful girl to get married and live happily ever after.*
And if you think **that's** *all a bit complicated, you should read the* **rest** *of the Mabinogion!*

The Water Monster of Brynberian
Not far from Brynberian, on the moorland of Presely, there is a prehistoric burial chamber called Bedd-yr-Afanc. In Welsh the word **afanc** *means either a beaver or a water monster of a horrifying kind. Welsh folk tales make it clear that it was sometimes huge and hairy, sometimes taking on a human form, and sometimes either a dwarf or a water horse. Tradition relates that the Brynberian* **afanc** *was caught in a pool near Brynberian Bridge and was afterwards taken up and buried in its stone grave on the mountain-side.*

EATING IN

While in Pembrokeshire, why not try your hand at some traditional local recipes? There are hundreds to choose from, and they are well described in a number of Welsh cookery books.

Among the best-known local savoury dishes are **Cawl** (Broth), usually made with bacon or beef and leeks, cabbage, carrots, potatoes and whichever vegetables are available. There are literally hundreds of variations on the theme with many local names. **Pastai Presely** (Presely Pie) was made with bacon, lean meat, and potatoes as a pie filling. **Faggots** are still extremely popular all over Pembrokeshire, made with pig's liver, breadcrumbs, sage and onions. They can be bought at most butcher's shops, and are ready cooked. All you have to do is to reheat them and serve with gravy and peas. Laver Bread (**Bara Lawr**) is greatly prized in Pembrokeshire, although there is now little commercial harvesting of the seaweed *Porphyra laciniata* by local seaside communities. Laver bread is not too pretty to look at, but do try it! (If you find it hard to stomach you can mix it with oatmeal and fold in an egg before frying it with fat; serve with fried bacon for breakfast or with boiled potatoes as an evening meal.)

Barafundle Bay

Fish dishes are very popular with Pembrokeshire folk, when there's fish to be had. Pickled and salted herrings, once part of the staple diet of coastal communities, are hard to come by these days, but there is plenty of mackerel on sale if you happen to be in the right place at the right time. Sewin is – in my humble opinion – infinitely superior to salmon; try it baked, with boiled Pembrokeshire early potatoes, broad beans, and parsley sauce. As for shellfish, cockles, mussels and limpets are all abundant if you know where to look and if you feel like trying a traditional Pembrokeshire shellfish pie.

There are many splendid local recipes for bread, cakes and puddings. Typically Welsh is **Bara Brith** (Speckled Bread) made with marmalade, mixed fruit, and (in some districts) half a pint of warm tea! **Teisennau Crwn** (Welsh Cakes), which can be baked either beneath a grill or on a bakestone, are of course tea-time favourites within and beyond the boundaries of Wales. **Bara Ceirch** (Oatcake) was popular all over Pembrokeshire, and Pembrokeshire Buns (**Miogod Sir Benfro**) were traditionally associated with New Year's Day celebrations. The small buns, known as *cace*, were given by householders to children as part of their *calennig* or New Year's Gift. Another tradional north county dish was **Poten Dato** (Potato Cake), made during the autumn when potatoes were plentiful. As a summer pudding, try the extremely delicious **Mwyar Duon** (Blackberry Pudding), made with white bread, blackberries and fresh cream.

EATING OUT

Pembrokeshire is full of excellent restaurants, and many pubs and inns are renowned for their fine meals also. If you are looking for inexpensive meals and good value for money there are cafés specialising in family meals in all the main towns and villages and even in some quite unexpected locations. For example, a number of popular tourist attractions have their own cafés. Try Pembroke Unicorn Carvery, the Castle Kitchen in Cilgerran, Keeston Kitchen near Simpson Cross, the Old Pharmacy in Solva, or the Dinas Diner at Dinas Cross. If you are looking for a special afternoon tea, try Cornerways Cream Teas at Simpson Cross. For evening meals we recommend Cnapan Restaurant at Newport, Jemima's Restaurant at Freystrop, the Trewern Arms on the riverside at Nevern, and Robeston House in Robeston Wathen. Also, many of the hotels and inns which advertise in this Guide have excellent restaurants.

CILGERRAN

Licensed Restaurant
Telephone: Cardigan 615055

Open every day for Cream Teas and Lunches
Evening Meals by Booking
Traditional British Good Food

Also Crafts, Paintings, Prints
and old Photographs
Close to Cilgerran Castle and Teifi Gorge

The Old Pharmacy

Licensed Restaurant

SOLVA

Speciality Seafood and Grills
with a friendly atmosphere

★ **ACCOMMODATION** ★

For Reservations
Telephone: (0437) 721232

We hope you have enjoyed your stay in Pembrokeshire. If so, and you run your own company, consider the feasibility of re-locating your business in this beautiful corner of Wales.

The MILFORD HAVEN WATERWAY ENTERPRISE ZONE offers small businessmen and bigger industrialists alike plenty of scope for development and prosperity including:-

ASSISTED AREA STATUS • SUPERB ENVIRONMENT • TAX & RATE BENEFITS · AMPLE FACTORY SPACE & DEVELOPMENT LAND (INCLUDING WATERFRONT SITES) • IDEAL FACILITIES FOR MARINE, LEISURE, GENERAL INDUSTRIAL & FOOD PROCESSING ACTIVITIES.

Find out more - contact the Zone Managers

•PEMBROKESHIRE BUSINESS INITIATIVE•

Pier House, Pier Road, Hobbs Point, Pembroke Dock, Dyfed SA72 6TR. Tel: Pembroke (0646) 684914.

WHERE BUSINESS IS A PLEASURE